A Collection of Collections

A COLLECTION
OF COLLECTIONS

BLACK | AMERICAN | POETRY

JOHN F. DILWORTH II

NEW YORK

LONDON • NASHVILLE • MELBOURNE • VANCOUVER

A COLLECTION OF COLLECTIONS

Black American Poetry

Published in New York, New York, by Morgan James Publishing. Morgan James is a trademark of Morgan James, LLC. www.MorganJamesPublishing.com

All poetry by John F. Dilworth II @johnfdilworth

All photography by Carlos York @chancelor__11

Proudly distributed by Ingram Publisher Services.

Morgan James BOGO™

A **FREE** ebook edition is available for you or a friend with the purchase of this print book.

CLEARLY SIGN YOUR NAME ABOVE

Instructions to claim your free ebook edition:
1. Visit MorganJamesBOGO.com
2. Sign your name CLEARLY in the space above
3. Complete the form and submit a photo of this entire page
4. You or your friend can download the ebook to your preferred device

ISBN 9781631956614 paperback
ISBN 9781631956621 ebook
Library of Congress Control Number:
2021939699

Cover Concept by:
Chris Treccani
www.3dogcreative.net

Cover and Interior Design by:
Chris Treccani
www.3dogcreative.net

Morgan James PUBLISHING
Builds
with...
Habitat for Humanity
Peninsula and Greater Williamsburg

Morgan James is a proud partner of Habitat for Humanity Peninsula and Greater Williamsburg. Partners in building since 2006.

Get involved today! Visit MorganJamesPublishing.com/giving-back

Dedicated to Atlanta, Georgia—USA

CONTENTS

PREFACE

2020 was one of the years that you wouldn't start talking about by saying it was "one of those years" because we've never seen anything like it. The year the world turned upside down and when it turned right side up again, so much had been rearranged that things didn't really look the same. Same stuff, it just looked and felt different and included a bunch of new norms. Now it seems like there's less gray area and more stark contrasts and either—or choices. Microphones have been given to the voiceless and the voteless and we hear you.

I remember New Year's Eve in 1999 when fear of Y2K chaos peppered the wind bringing in the year 2000. I wonder if that would have been worse than COVID-19. I wonder if poetry could have been the vaccine.

This is the sharing of perspective. It's the cure for polarization, partisanship, and prejudice. When we get a glimpse of things from someone else's perspective, understanding (or at least empathy) occurs more organically. This is me challenging you to see things through mine and find something you can use as you look beyond the surface. You are more than red or blue like I am more than black or white or right or left. No matter how much they try to break life down to 1's and 0's, there is simply more to it than that and there always will be. Love is the X factor and the Y is humanity and hate is just... hate. Too often we choose it over actually sitting down and talking with each other or sharing a poem or book or recipe or photograph. And this is the sharing of perspective because poetry just may be the vaccine.

These selected poems from the years 2000 through 2020 should be plenty. They are from the first 21 years of the 21st century which has been tumultuous indeed. In that time frame personally, I became a man, got married and divorced, traveled the world, lost all of my grandparents and my father, started my business, went broke, gained a life partner, discovered my purpose and so much more. I have no doubt that (as unique as my experience has been) it is not so unique. We all have been through a lot and more connects us than divides us despite all the walls and barriers and stigmas that we are forced to live amongst. We have seen the USA's first black president, its first female vice president, the 9-11 attacks, wildfires on the west coast, war in Iraq, mass shootings in schools, bars, even churches, Hurricane Katrina, climate change, bold defense of white supremacy, the Black Lives Matter movement, and yes— the Covid-19 pandemic. We didn't get to pick and choose which controversial issues we discussed, or what battles we fought. No matter what your ideology or religion or gender or race or sexual orientation or age or how deep your pockets were or how smart you thought you were—we were all in this thing together. We *are* all in this thing together.

So, use this as an opportunity to walk a mile in someone else's shoes. Try actually listening to what someone else has to say. Have a desire to understand and be willing to open up your heart to your husband or wife or parent or child or coworker or total stranger. How about that person you swore you would never talk to again? What about your perceived enemy? Because we are all in this thing together, and this is the sharing of perspective, and poetry just may be the vaccine.

LOVIN' AIN'T EASY

In a Place Where (Lovin' Ain't Easy)

Hard times
Take tolls on soft bodies
Soon to be calloused
By experience
By tough love
Found solely in the streets
Of midnight madness
Daytime drama
Police lights
Junkies high as kites
Kinky-haired single mothers
Who came up on the same block of concrete
Where
Lovin' ain't easy
But it still gets done
Even though sometimes you gotta run
Sometimes you gotta stand your ground
In the place that makes the sun frown
And the moon cry
Tears of joy
Because it's still getting done
In a place where hot hearts
Turn cold
At thirteen years old
The businesses close early
Or stay open all night long
One extreme to the other
In a place where ashy legs
Patrol sidewalks
On worn soles
In a place where

Dope boys ride the cleanest
In an effort to inspire
The youth
And attract the hungry girls
In a place where
Lovin' ain't easy
But it still gets done.

Clockwork Hotfoot

Exit the MARTA rail and take a left towards the worksite
Did things a few hours ago that shouldn't be done on a work night
But still ready to take on the new day just like yesterday
Heard the crew say they can't take anymore
This job is a revolving door
Everybody's a minority except for the employer
Walking to work to clock in right past the lawyer
But Hotfoot won't complain
Out loud
Hotfoot stand out from the crowd
Arrive early leave early
Got moonlighting to do
Elbow grease and midnight oil too
Want different do different
Do more and say less
Like clockwork with the dreams
The superiors ain't supreme
Focus is
Determination is
A made-up mind is
Making heaven out of hell
A right from the worksite right back to the MARTA rail.

Time has Wings

My oh my
How Time does fly
My granddaddy told me
I would understand better by and by
So I try to cherish every moment
And appreciate the little things
Because one thing I can't deny
Is that Time has wings
And she spreads them in steady flight
Time never stands still
She's constantly giving birth
But look at all she's managed to kill
Vivid dreams and mighty kings
Have seen the edge of her sword
Taking Time for granted
Is a luxury none of us can afford
Underestimating her prowess
Is a sure path to defeat
But making her an ally
Makes you so much harder to beat
They say time heals all wounds
And she outlasts the many moons
And outlasts the sunshine
She's seen so many noons
And been the topic of so many tunes
The elephant in so many rooms
She thwarted so many attempts
To be swept away by so many brooms
And my oh my
How Time does fly
My granddaddy told me

I would understand better by and by
So I try to cherish every moment
And appreciate the little things
Like an angel in the sky
Or an eagle flying high
One thing I can't deny
Is that Time has wings.

Sacrifice

I never claimed to be a philosopher or intellectual giant
To be politically correct or politically defiant
But somehow or another I've come by some information
To perplex and confound this system's education
Of misappropriated priorities and brainwashed imagination
It's a supernatural anomaly an unsolvable equation
The most important thing I've learned in my development and
maturation
Is that sacrifice is love's greatest manifestation
"For God so loved the world that he gave His only begotten Son"
Abraham was ready to offer Isaac just to see God's will be done

I never said I was a genius or the wisest one in all the land
But when I learned this lesson, I truly learned to be a man
Sacrifice is required when I must truly prove my love
If they're not willing to sacrifice for you, they weren't sent from
above
So when you don't know if it's real and you need some
authentication
Consider this: sacrifice is love's greatest manifestation
"For God so loved the world that he gave His only begotten Son"
What would you do if God asked you to give up your only one?

I never said that I was perfect or have it all figured out
That's never been my style, that's not what I'm about
But somehow or another I've come by this information
That somehow or another has evaded the general population
Even Christian folk who are supposed to be trying to live like
Christ
Will go to great extremes just to avoid sacrifice
Some of us have forgotten that it's better to give than to receive
But that statement is easier to say than it is to practice and
believe
But what about the crown of thorns that was pressed on my
Savior's head?
What about when He could have saved Himself but suffered
for us instead?
What about the pure and innocent blood that was unjustly
allowed to spill?
What about that rugged cross that Jesus carried up that hill?
It was His sacrifice that prepared the way for my salvation
And somehow or another I've come by this information
Which is the most important thing I've learned in my
development and maturation
Sacrifice is love's greatest manifestation.

All People

We're all just people
Working together
Working against each other
Living together
Living apart
Loving
And hating

And having it all
Having a ball
And suffering
Through happiness and pain
Striving
For more
Hurting for more
And I am no exception.

Widow's Peak

Sometimes he just hits me
Sometimes he chokes me
Sometimes he throws me on the floor
Sometimes I fall hard enough for the neighbors to hear me
next door
When I met him, he was a sailor in a crispy uniform
When I looked into his eyes, it looked as if he would take the
world by storm
He walked with so much pride and he drove a fancy car
He said he wanted to take me for a ride and promised not to
go too far
And ever since then, I loved that man
But when I went to sleep, in my dreams, I pushed and shoved
that man
'Cause when he's had too much liquor and he comes through
that door
Sometimes I fall hard enough for the neighbors to hear me
next door
'Cause sometimes he throws me on the floor
Sometimes he just slaps me in my face
'Cause he's on probation and just caught another case

Because he got the "I'll call you back speech" at the job
interview
And when I ask him "how are you going to deal with the pain"
He says "I'll take it out on you"
His father abused his mother and before long, left them alone
And he never knew his father well but looks just like his clone
He's a fallen angel, he's a king who lost his crown
But when I try to pull him up, all he does is beat me down
But how much more can I take, how much more can I stand for
'Cause sometimes I fall hard enough for the neighbors to hear
me next door
Sometimes he just throws me on the floor
Sometimes he slams me against the wall
'Cause he's six foot one, and I'm only five feet tall
The last time he came home too drunk, he fractured my right
arm
But that's his third time hurting me bad, and the third time is
the charm
So now I got me a new friend, his name is Calico .38
And I load him with lead tears as I sit here and wait
For him to have too much liquor and walk through that door
And I'll make sure he never throws me on the floor anymore.

Nobody Knows

Nobody knows that I fasted
Nobody knows that I prayed
Nobody knows that I worked
So much harder than I played
All they know is that I prevailed
In whatever game it was that I played.

A King's Thoughts About His Queen
(As He Sits in Deliberation)

Real love
Is birthed through situation
It undeniably precedes us
But takes maturation
And some seeds never grow
Some seeds get halfway
But fall victim to the snow
But ours is manifesting
Into something that I could never know
Hard-earned and superior
To my previous self
Not reaching for the rewards of my previous wealth
But reaching beyond the premises of the cloud
Which is only a perceived limitation
Real love
Is birthed through situation
I won't deny it
Has taken patience with myself
Because my learning pattern has been repetitive
Learning to extract positive from the numerical negative
That must be overcome
To build a kingdom
And the queen is the most valuable piece to the king on his
board
And losing that queen the king can ill afford
Which could be deadly
So the authenticity of the love must be factored in heavily
And Real love
Is birthed through situation
Battle tested when critical yet still standing

In validation
Certified and qualified by meeting all prerequisites
Because winning is not a given
It must be earned
Not blinded by the depiction of winning society perpetuates
in their description
Which causes some to copy dreams but not account for the
ambition
But we put our heads together and try to hold up this shield
Striving for excellence through the hues of blues and black
Through the track that we trek and trailblaze to a new
elevation
Regardless of circumstance we move in the direction of
deliberate destination
Real love
Is birthed through situation.
A king's thoughts about his queen as he sits in deliberation…

Life Is Over Before You Know It

Somebody hip me to some game
They said life is over before you know it
So take what you got on the inside
And try your best to show it
Don't hold it
Because if you do, you'll regret it in the end
Somewhere drunk off in a corner
Pondering on what you could have been
It's all within
And it never had a chance to be known
When you were a kid
You said that you would be successful when you got grown

But time moved on
Just a little bit faster than you thought
Time is money
And with your time, the wrong things were bought
So you fought
Like a boxer trying to come back in the 12th round
But your eye was already cut
And your mouthpiece was on the ground
And now you're getting all your children's clothing
From the church's lost-and-found
And your baby momma or baby daddy
Hardly ever comes around
You don't want to drown
So you struggle to keep your head above water
But you're getting tired and you're getting weak
And the struggle is only getting harder
Somebody hip me to some game
They said life is over before you know it
So take what you got on the inside
And try your best to show it
Don't throw it
All away before you get your time to shine
Stay ahead in the race
And you won't have to worry about being behind
That's the bottom line
But it's thin like skating on late February ice
Sometimes you only get one chance
You're lucky if you go twice
Sacrifice
The needless things and aim for a higher goal
Stick to the script
Don't keep trying to change your role
Potholes and puddles of mud

Will always be in the road
So plan ahead, expect the unexpected
And pack a lighter load
Take what you got on the inside
And try your best to show it
Somebody hip me to some game
They said life is over before you know it.

Precious Baby Girl

He laid restless in the belly of his mother to be
Turning and kicking
Anxious to see
The light of the world
But how was this baby boy going to be raised by this baby girl
He was seven months and she was seventeen
But neither could imagine the future's heartaches unseen
She confessed that some nights she cried herself to sleep
And tried to hide her pregnancy, but it was a hard secret to keep
When the tenth month came, the labor was induced
And she screamed from the top of her lungs from the pain that
it produced
Thirteen hours of breathing and pushing in the maternity ward
She said it was at this moment that she felt closest to the Lord
And when it was all over, on her face, she wore a smile
Because she was finally able to hold in her arms her newborn
infant child
Who once laid restless in her belly anxious to see
The light of the world
But how was this little baby boy going to be raised by this
precious baby girl?
She swore she would face the challenge and be a model mother

But there were so many lessons she had not learned, so many
things she had yet to discover
She worked and went to school and tried the best she could
While he was being raised without a father-figure and this is
never good
If not detrimental
The baby's daddy refused to raise the child because the
pregnancy was accidental
The boy was another one so reckless with unprotected sex
So it could've been worse
She could've gotten AIDS, plus she stopped smoking cigarettes
For her, things may not have had to go the way they went
She wouldn't be in that predicament had she waited until she
shed some vulnerabilities
But then she would not yet have this child
Who once laid restless in her belly
Anxious to see
The light of the world
But how was this little baby boy going to be raised by this
precious baby girl?

The Other Side of the Other Side

I was born on the other side of the other side
Oh, I'll tell you how to get there
Just make a left at nowhere
Then make a right at wrong
And you'll find my home
My home squared
My full circle with four corners
And corn flakes and cabbage patches
Blacktops and droptops

High stocks and cash crops
A lot of niggas and a few father figures
Triggers and paper figures
Blood diamond diggers and misquoted scriptures
And that's just the front yard
Welcome
To the other side of the other side
Make yourself at home but take your shoes off
And you might not want snooze off
Or doze off
Go in the back room if you want to take your clothes off
And after that, if you're feeling dirty
Of course, you can always hose off
The Cadillac is king and we name our babies Mercedes
They slowed down on making ladies in the early eighties
So now it ain't the same
And nobody's tame
Oh, I'm sorry
You said you're ready to leave?
No, you should stay a while
The sun ain't went down
So you got a while before it gets wild
I understand, you really must be getting on
Well, I'll tell you how to get out
When you get to wrong, make a left
And when you get nowhere, make a right
And you'll find your home.

To Striving Lovers of God and Each Other:

I feel us about to win
It's happening again
I feel us about to see success
I don't have to guess
Though I don't know exactly what is next
I've already seen it in my dream manifested context
Nevertheless, it's forming
Like a regenerated man of steel in an incubator
Stationed on an ascension elevator
I feel us about to win
And we win together
It may be possible without but with is much better
So we build
On solid spiritual estate
So success is fate
There will be debate
As situations escalate
But we stand together
We win together
There is a strong glue in this chemistry
And accurate telemetry
Through measurements of Faith
And now I'm saving grace
While simultaneously running the race
Amazed because I don't have to adjust my pace
To see your face
You're in my space
But you only add to its capacity
When it comes to the matter of winning.

Pride

Pride will put you in a box
Secured with locks
That others have the keys to
And the only way to let them release you
Is to surrender your own pride
White-flagged and peaceful
Humble is the way
To avoid being your own prey
Or a prisoner to what you say
Be mindful and in control of what you display
And leave open for interpretation
Vulnerable to attack and interrogation
Negative exposure and humiliation
Be low
And they can never bring you down
Or cause you to drown
In your own pride.

Along the Way

I have hurt people along the way
And I wish I didn't hurt them
I have loved people along the way
And I wish I didn't love them so hard
Not because loving hard is wrong
But because loving hard can consume you
And swallow you up
If you let it

And I let it
Love is a slippery slope
An insurmountable climb
Sour and sweet like a lime
Perfection at your fingertips
But never in your clutch.

25

I'm 25 and still alive
Exercising inadvertent actions
Like breathing, blinking, and dreaming
Seeming to be more than meets the eye
Because some thought that I
Was nothing more than an aimless pedestrian
But I am an equestrian
Riding life stallions down rocky roads
And unbeaten paths
Hopefully, I haven't seen the half
Or even the better half of the two halves
But if I have
That's alright because
I'm 25 and still alive
In a place where
I should've got shot by now
I should've got got by now
I should not have seen a lot by now
But I've seen war and I've seen peace
From America to the Middle East
Will the chaos ever cease?
Drama poppin' off like hot grease in the streets
Leaves young men and young women deceased in the streets

They're no longer alive
They'll never see 25
I thought the streets were supposed to teach us to survive
Well why are there so many casualties?
Moralities have become abnormalities
The truth's been replaced with fallacies
Souls have been traded for salaries
Even quality of life is attached to a price
And that's supposed to be a civil right
I swear to God—it ain't right
The way they make us fight for stinking bite
Of this pie while they're born with their mouths stuffed with a
free slice
What they need, we need twice
Maybe even three times
A-town down, now I'm stuck throwing these peace signs
When I know these ain't no peace times
And somehow or another

I'm 25 and still alive
But it was only recently that I really started living
It was only recently that I really stopped giving
A dang about these temporal things so that I could be free
I stopped trying to conform to this world
I'll make this world conform to me and G.O.D.
They thought the hood was all I knew
They thought my eyes were stuck to the TV like
You are stuck to these words
But I took their stereotypes and proved them wrong with these
words
I speak spoken words but if I were to rap

It wouldn't be about movin' keys and hustlin' birds
It would be about turning keys and being birds
Flying high up in the sky
I mean literally being birds
Now my eye view
Allows me to see visions
That motivate me to try to
Make them manifest
And this is my greatest test
But I must confess that I am blessed
Because

I'm 25 and still alive
Exercising inadvertent actions
Like sneezing, hearing, and thinking
Responding
Reacting
Protracting the truth
Impacting the youth
In ways so powerfully positive that even if negative values were
added
They still wouldn't be less than zero
Which makes me equivalent to or greater than a hero
Now we go 'round and 'round until this cycle is broken
I'm trying to get you traveling in a new direction
Like an ol' school MARTA token
I ain't joking
I'm just hoping that these words are soaking
Or maybe even poking holes in your intellect
Permuting possibilities
Permeating principle

Tearing down the lies and making their system of none effect
I've got a gift that I can't neglect
So even when these times are hard
I am thanking God
Because
I'm 25 and still alive.

Untitled

My diamonds were shining so bright
It made her lose track of time
And while she was glancing at my wrist
I was digging into her mine
And I wasn't looking for coal
I was looking for gold
She tried to fit into my mold
But that's a story already told
So that's already old
When I'm onto something new
Like I saw a tainted canvas and discovered a new shade of blue
Though I'm big on green
Trying to leave a lasting impression like tee shirts from silk screen
Or the brightest light you've ever seen
It's more than meets the eye like measurements from triple beam
Scales not big enough to handle the weight of my dream
It made her want to scream
And cry tears of joy again
But that's a twisted nightmare that she doesn't want to rebegin
A king and a queen
Don't always go together
But like an optimistic pessimist, you can never say never.

Crazy Timing

You came at crazy timing
But I never wrote a love poem to a trap song
Until you came along
Unique name and strong
Standing there at the entrance of the path that leads to throne
Not mine alone
For the masses
For the classes
As I navigate through different classes
And you're right there when I pass this
Which can be applied to different scenarios
You met my mama
And saw all my drama
Almost went under in my thunder
As I carve up this river
To sail on
I can see it
And the more I can see it, the more I accept it as reality
You showed me the way to dream and still remember when I
wake up
I can better spot the real the more I learn these shades of
makeup
Some want to see the tinman break up
Into a bunch of little pieces
So it's better to be a lion
It's better to be a lioness
Watching my back in the den
Correcting the scars from my skin
All in amazing fashion
Dancing

Strolls and pirouettes
Big smiles and rolled eyes
Young but wise
Wise but naïve as the wild night that turns to day
Past the allotment of time to play
You sure are lovely
You sure are, Lovely
And I know it's hard to trust me
But you trust me
And I don't take that lightly
The fairy tale likely
Not motivated by what it might be
But motivated by what it is
I immediately associated you with diamonds
The way you were shining
And you came at crazy timing
Like Robin coming to save Batman just before the vice rips
him apart
And you carry my heart
Not because my stroke is the best
I just woke up blessed
To find you here
After many moons of howling
And staying in the race even when my stomach's growling
No honey in the cupboards
No easy way for the lovers
No explore no discover
You sleep under my cover
But you're the face of the franchise
The secret to all the sauce
And I love you
A lot less than you know above you
You looked in my mirror and it was you

Beautiful even when you didn't like to hear it
Like I heard it in spirit
And I never wrote a love poem to a trap song
Until you came along
Shining bright like a diamond
You came at crazy timing.

What I Lost

I lost my father and lost my money
And I can only get one back
So now I have no choice
But to focus and grind and stack
I was built for the adversity
Built to survive in each transition
I have my father's patience
I have my mother's ambition
So I continue to live my life
In a constant state of appreciation
Abased that I may abound
The spiritual path to elevation
My life is a skyscraper
And I came in on the ground floor
I've been down in the dark before
And still found my way through the door...

I lost my marriage and lost my seed
Though I sowed on fertile ground
Been around the world and back again
I've been lost and I've been found
My life is a movie
An unscripted unfinished story

And in my Oscar acceptance speech
I'll give God all the glory
I won't hide what He is doing
I'll share my testimony
So you can call me whatever you want
Just please don't call me phony
And I know my dad is with me
Each and every step of the way
Just as sure as he came home from work
After each and every day
Like the sunrise every morning
He will come to see me shine
With the spirits of courage and excellence
Through this most difficult time.

You Still Love Me

I love You, Lord
Even through all my discombobulations
Separations from general populations
Reintegrations, situations, and maturations
I still love You
Even through my fluctuations
Incarcerations and liberations
Degradations and elevations, losses, and tribulations
You still love me, Lord
When I let You down
When friends stop coming around
When I was broken and about to drown
You still love me
As my faith has evolved
And the world has revolved

While my progress was paused
And I floated in my flaws
You never stopped loving me
And I never stopped loving You.

Modern-Day Warfare: Lovin' was Never Easy

Lovin' was never easy
But it still had to get done
Love was always a battlefield
A fight that had to be won
Imagine: being a slave
Trying your best to be brave
But your woman is owned by another man
While you're treated like a man from a cave
But you were born to be a provider
You were born to be a protector
And you stand and fight for love
When it's so easy to be a defector
The last thing you want to do
Is wave the white flag
It wasn't easy being a husband
It wasn't easy being a dad
When your fight was all you had
For the woman, it was just as bad
Imagine: being invaded by a man that you don't love
You hate him and he hates you back
He hates you because you're black
But when ain't nobody looking
He loves to lay you on your back
You want to be a queen to your king
But they convinced you that your king doesn't exist

So you conform to a way of thinking
That's completely devilish
And it's carried on through generations
Passed on through the life of the seed
Now that's biological warfare
Genetically engineered to replace generosity with greed
A divide and conquer strategy
They don't want your love to survive
Because love makes you strong
Love compels you to strive

Now flash forward to today
Love is still under attack
You gotta fight to keep your love
'Cause when you lose it, it's hard to get it back
And it's modern-day warfare
Man against the machines
Artificial intelligence
More real than it actually seems
Virtual reality
Have you chasing manipulated dreams
Have you using love as a means
To carry out materialistic schemes
Twerkin' for a Birkin
Love is now for sale
So much fake love available
That when it's real, it's hard to really tell
You gotta camouflage your emotions
To make it harder for the snipers
You can't walk in the grass barefooted
If you want to protect your soles from the vipers
Skinny girl wanna be thicker
Fat girl wanna be slim

Posting pics all on her page
Going hard up in the gym
Motivated by the likes
But still somebody's throwing shade
When you let down your walls of defense
The enemy throws over a grenade
Now she's sharing selfies of her and her hubby
Somewhere on a beach
Hugged up all lovey-dovey
But envy is lurking on her timeline
And she's just making her moves easier to study
Now it's going down in his DM
And she's suspicious, so he's scared to leave his phone
Now they are both prisoners of war
That allowed the enemy to infiltrate their home

And lovin' was never easy
But it still had to get done
But now the battlefield is different
And the war is seldom won
Divorce has become the norm
And so many children are born
With only one parent
Because the household was divided and torn
Before they even arrived
Imagine: being a child
Learning how to love
In these times that are so wild
And you walk into your parents' bedroom
And see your father being bent over the bed
And as you form your thoughts on manhood
That image is in your head
This is modern day warfare

But the fight ain't fair
How did the fabric of a man
Become so easy to tear
Love was always a burden
But now, so few are stronger enough to bare
Or grounded enough to care
Now it's all about the optics
Taking pics in front of Rolls Royces
Or lounging in Lamborghini cockpits
And the picture ain't right if it's not a trophy wife
You're flying first class and private
To show the world a trophy life
That you may or may not live
But it's all you've got to give
Morally bankrupt
Ran out of f*#ks to give
And you're all about your coins
You just wanna secure the bag
But before you secure the bag
You prematurely start to brag
'Cause it's the most you ever had
But it's not everything you need
Remember the part where I said
They replaced generosity with greed?
The trickery is so prickly
And it'll poke you without you knowing
Trying to flex on everybody else
But weakness is all you're showing
Imagine: being a man
With no concept of self-worth
So you're defined by what you can buy
That's what you want people to see first
So you decide to protect your pride

By letting no one see what's beneath the surface
Without realizing that lack of love
Is the reason you feel so worthless
Love defines your purpose
But love is constantly under attack
You gotta fight to keep your love
'Cause in this modern-day warfare
When you lose it, it's hard to get it back.

MESSAGES OF LOST HOPE

You Don't Lose Until You Quit

Setbacks have come my way on this highway
But it's better than the low way
It's better than looking at my challenges and saying "no way"
It's better than looking at opportunity and saying "I'll never make it through that doorway"
I just can't settle for the sure way
There's no easy way on this hard road but the hard road leads to high places
Though sometimes it might lead through wet tears onto dry faces
But I guess that's why hope leads to faith after experience leads to patience
And I must live as an example
Therefore, I cannot allow my dreams to be trampled
So when I face obstacles beyond my strength, God helps me overcome what I can't handle
He's my guiding light when these harsh winds blow out my candle
He's the foundation on which I stand while so many others choose to sit
But maybe they give up because they don't know that you don't lose until you quit
Just keep pushing and keep going when it's raining and when it's snowing
When the earth is quaking and the ground is shaking
When your world is flooding and your heart is breaking
Joy will come in the morning, no matter how long the sun is taking
Victory is sweet but defeat produces a bitter blend
And the race is not given to the swift but he who endures to the end

For me, the danger of dying is more acceptable than the shame
of giving in
I just hope you're receiving the message that I am trying to send
Because when I focus on my purpose, my passion takes over
the fight
And yes, it's a heavy burden but it's filled with so much light
It's filled with so much value, it's filled so much worth
And we all have purpose of our own that we've been carrying
since birth
And that's the foundation on which I stand while so many
others choose to sit
But maybe they give up because they just don't know that you
don't lose until you quit
It's not over until it's over, go on revise that business plan
Stand up for what you believe, be a woman, be a man
Keep applying for that job, keep taking that test until you pass
Keep studying, keep grinding, keep refusing to settle for last
Keep working towards that future, keep building on those dreams
Keep your focus and keep your peace amidst the chaos, cries
and screams
Because no excuse will be accepted and failure is not an option
Don't listen to naysayers because they want to see you stopping
They want to see you stooping to their low levels of
expectation
But you an achiever, a superseder of situation
And if these words are motivation then I am your relation
Not by blood but by struggle with like faith and like
foundation
On which we choose to stand while so many others choose to sit
Because we know and understand that you don't lose until you
quit.

Modern Abolitionist

I am a modern abolitionist trying to break slavery's chains
But no longer do they whip us, they just put nooses around
our brains
A container is only as valuable as the substance it contains
For so many years our cup's contents have been poured down
the drains
Pain is all that remains once the cup is empty
But having my glass full doesn't exempt me
From all this countries restrictions and burdens on my back
'Cause most of the legislators are white and small percentage
of them are black
The probation officer is on the attack and on my track like
bloodhounds
But I counteract methodically like a gatling gun with verbal
rounds
Like a forgotten abolitionist in the modern days of a different
kind
Fighting the good fight against genocide of the mind
This race always takes a step forward then sits down and falls
behind
As if we were walking in the darkness or in the light, but just
blind
But this is the rebirth of Ben Mays and Fred Douglass
Intellectuals amongst savages living lawless and loveless

I am a modern abolitionist trying to break the chains of slavery
But when will my brothers stop mistaking stupidity for bravery
And it's not some white man's fault wholly and completely

Because in actuality we keep ourselves from being free
He tried so hard to be hard that his heart felt like a brick
So I came to him with new thoughts through ideological
rhetoric
As if I were giving teaspoons of medicine to a child that was sick
I told him that lies are unnecessary but truth is intrinsic
You can't bend it, you can only bring it to the light
You can't ignore your wings forever, you eventually have to
take flight
Or be drowned by the plight which is a biproduct of lack of
insight
Why are you walking around with your eyes closed tight
But on the other hand the other man only makes matters worse
They tried to imbed in our heads that being born black is
being born under a curse
From the day of our birth
They tried to tell us that we're inferior and our lives have less
worth
And now they try to tell us that they don't feel the same way
But their actions don't reflect some of the things that they say
The game is just played a different way
They lay you off from your job so when you get evicted you
won't have a place to stay
Now forced to live your life with no shelter from the rains
While they erect big expensive buildings using big expensive
cranes
And they no longer whip us, they just put nooses around our
brains
But I am a modern abolitionist trying to break slavery's chains.

What Do You Call Home?

Manic depression grabbed hold of my folk
Strung out on cigarettes and indo smoke
Enough to make that old man choke
Like he had a bone in his throat
And I done seen po' kids that'll eat anything they find like a
billy goat
These words you may choose not to quote
True as they may be
And sometimes I wish I could build a boat and not look back
as I cross the sea
But I gotta stay down to promote unity amongst the people
like me
Black as the eye in the black-eyed pea
Brown as the dirt used to create the first man
Strong but at the same time naïve like herds of cattle
So where do find the balance in that
The way they do our lives made Marvin Gaye wanna holler, it
makes me want to scream
But instead I hold it in and find myself subjected to tossing
and turning when I dream
Until awakened by a sunbeam
Peeking through my windows
And the sound of leaves rustling in trees when the wind blows
But sometimes the world is silent like the sound the ground
makes when it comes in contact with the snow
Then it gets louder as it gets trampled on
From the 4 ward to the 3 zone
Where some will grind hard and save all their money just to
ride on chrome
Now what do you call home?

Atlanta, Georgia
New York or Florida
Some say the world is a ghetto
But what about the mountains and the meadow
The plains and the plateau
Do they feel my pain
If they did, would it drive them insane
To hear this noise in the concrete jungle
Better ride extra precautious in robbing season which lasts all
year long
Now what do you call home?

Atlanta, Georgia or Little Rock
Los Angeles or D. C.
Society where nothing comes for free
I never knew anybody from Beverly Hills or Rodeo Drive
But I know some folks who took that New Jersey Drive and
hustled to stay alive
Never saw the shine of a silver spoon
Never ate lunch every day at noon
They just walked the streets bobbing their heads to the hungry
man's tune
Hoping it'll all be over soon
And I'm subjected to tossing and turning when I dream
Because this so-called American dream gets clouded by this
American scheme
To get us caught up in the system as they privatize the jails
We're in an age where information travels at the speed of light,
but our progress is slow like snails
'Cause we're still gang banging
And it's not from trees, but we're still hanging
Chaining ourselves to the wall

Covering our own ears so we can't hear the battle cry or the
warning call
Roll the dice against the wall and hope you don't crap out
'Cause when they get ya in that position where you can't do
anything all you can do is tap out
Manic depression grabbed hold of my folk
And I done seen po' kids that'll eat anything they find like a
billy goat
And some built that boat but got to the middle of the sea
before they realized it wouldn't float
Now stranded in the waters of the metropolis
Fighting against the waves of hypocrisy strong as a
hippopotamus
But we're on the rise and there's no stopping us
From my city to yours
These conditions carry on
Now what do you call home?

Atlanta, Georgia, Houston, Texas
Detroit or Chicago
Where the money comes fast but that's the same way it go
Oh, I'm surprised you didn't know
Some say the world is a ghetto
But I don't think they feel my pain in the mountains and the
meadow
The plains and the plateau
Our children are being raised in the depths of an ominous
shadow
Our water wells are shallow
'Cause the boys are growing up without fathers and it's still
cool to slang dope
But I come with Messages of Lost Hope
To replace the Inner-City Blues

Another man gets killed on Simpson Street;
but it wasn't on the evening news
I try hard not get frustrated and confused
Because I must be available to be used in the way
the Lord wants me to be used
But these streets sometimes take on a mind of their own
Now what do you call home?

The End Could Come Before It Is Expected

I told him that the end could come before it is expected
So consider your future priceless and refuse to neglect it
Protect it
Participate in positive things and you'll find your time was well
invested
The generations before us protested
And got what they wanted by staying determined when they
were tested
Let the truth be manifested
We all need forgiveness, when I made mistakes, I confessed it
Before I closed my eyes when I laid down and rested
I've been a few places and seen a few things, I remember the
times I got arrested
At one point the system had left me mentally molested
All this smoke in the air can leave the mind congested
I told him that the end could come before it is expected
To get the answer to the question, the knowledge has to be
requested
A closed mouth won't get fed, in the dark the light won't be
reflected
The project will never be complete unless the foundation is
erected

And the right path is selected
Let movement be a disease and let your joints be infected
I can't stray from responsibility, as a leader—I've been elected
By the Almighty Who is the utmost respected
He gave me this message for you and in your blood, I must inject it
Your brain cells must detect it
And know that the end could come before it is expected.

My Head is Heavy

My head is heavy
I feel as if I'm about to break like a levy
The wages of war can be deadly
I am not weak
But I'm not so unique
I'm so ready to break this streak
Of losing
My heart can't take much more bruising
The pain is intruding
When it rains it pours
Even when indoors
And it's flooding my floors
But I've built up my walls
And filled empty halls
And bucked on the laws
That would hold me down
I refuse to drown
Or succumb to the sound
Of dripping
Though my hand is slipping
I hold on to my gripping

Until victory is mine
I'm not that far behind
The potential of my time
I'm a warrior at heart
My story is my art
So I'll keep it together
I won't fall apart.

An Idle Mind is the Workshop of the Devil

An idle mind is the workshop of the Devil
And it is that thought which brings me to this table
Able to vent my anxiousness through words instead of actions
Relaxing and allowing myself to remain free
And see that there's a right time and a right place for
everything
Anything can be accomplished if I first develop a plan
Understand myself and prioritize my goals
My holes have been filled with completion
Deletion of the spaces once left void
Now employed for determination
Obligation and potential to fulfill
Kill the dead and let life flourish
Nourish the mind, I am thankful to be still living
Giving a part of myself to my people
Equal under God's eyes
Let's utilize our instruments
In increments beyond measure of a number
Slumber wastes time, now take heed to the title
An idle mind is the workshop of the devil.

PUSH!

PUSH!
Be who you were created to be
Be what you were created to be
And don't settle for anything less
Regardless of the stress
No matter how long it takes
Or if your heart breaks
You are stronger than you think you are
But you won't know that strength
Without facing your perceived weakness
Head on

PUSH!!
Give birth to what you were created to create
But first you have to carry it
And bear the burden of that treasure
Even when the weight is more than you can measure
Impress yourself
Be awed by the prowess that you cultivate
Through pain and practice
It is worth it
You are worth it… push.

Revolution of the Mind

The room started spinning, but the Gin in the cabinet was left
untouched
I said the room started spinning, but the Gin in the cabinet
was left untouched

I was in a sober trance
Doing a dance without moving the legs in my pants
Enhanced by visions of the past combined with hopes for the
future
When Destiny crept in quietly and startled me, I almost
started to shoot her
Until she spoke these words "Peace be unto you
I come with lost messages a little different from the ones you're
used to
Because these messages are true
So many have deceived you, but I have perceived you to be
able to handle this mind-state that I bring"
And when she gave it to me, she told me to wear it with pride
like a gold medal or heirloom ring
Passed down from my great grandfather who lived when times
were harder
And I'll pass it on to my grandsons who'll say I lived when
times were harder
For starters, the police ride around in Impalas with twelve
gauges in their trunks
Ready to be aimed at my kinsmen whom they call young punks
But I call them street scholars, hungry and blinded by the
need for dollars
I call them my brothers
Being suffocated by the system's bloody pillow under injustice's
dirty covers
So preoccupied with the dog eat dog way of the world that
they find it hard to find time to be good lovers
Creating fatherless children while abandoning their mothers
But Destiny came to me with the Messages of Lost Hope
She told me to wash my mind clean with this gift of mental soap
Because my mind state had been tainted, soiled, and stained

She said "during hard times, don't just find a way to cope, find
a way to change
Rearrange and reclaim what has gotten so out of control"
She told me to feel it in my heart, she told me to plant it in
my soul
So that one day it might grow and strike its fist against the
judge who sentenced me without even looking in my eyes
"No respect for the man of color", I thought as my
temperature started to rise
And then I ripped away the disguise that had held my light in
for so long
Mind-state revolutionized, I sang a completely different song
Of the Messages of Lost Hope brought to me by Destiny
Who said the shackles and whips were gone, but there is still
mental slavery
And I cannot rest until every man can be a functioning part of
this society
Created in theory to be for you and for me
For my children and for yours
Whose only worry should be about getting a whooping for not
doing their chores
Instead of what are we going to eat and what are we going to
wear
Why can't we afford our own clothes, why do we have to share
Why doesn't daddy care, and speaking of daddy, can you tell
me where
He is in this day when we need his sunshine
Mommy, why do we have to stand in this welfare line for the
umpteenth time
But I've chosen to live in fast-forward instead of living in rewind
I've come to enjoy Destiny's gift of revolution of the mind.

This is Where the Moon Goes

So..
This is where the moon goes
It's up here at the top
When it disappears from my view
It's not as far away as it seemed
It's still doing its thing
When I lose sight of its inspiration
It's just an elevator ride away
In its own little hideaway
So I pay it a visit
From my humble abode
From the highs and the lows
And I leave reassured
Because I know it still glows.

Progress Awaits the Road

A new beginning has been taken
Now progress awaits the road
Born again like babies on their second life
The afterlife intrigues the guilty
And innocent as well
Heaven or Hell
Maybe the world will become a cell
And captivate all the hooligans and holy world sinners
Greedy big money spenders
Yea, maybe the world will become a cell
But who can tell
Knowledge is moved by the wind like a sail
Blowing through tides of experience and youth

Troubled as it may seem
They can't submerge my dream
Of moving to the next level continuously until the day that I die
Now progress awaits the road
I unload my aggression through pen on point like pin
Born again like babies on their second life
But not everybody gets that extra chance
So while I have the chance, I must advance
While maintaining a fearless soldier stance
Learning from my mistakes
Placing caution in the daily stride
All truth with nothing to hide
Except the emptiness inside
That will not subside until my dreams are satisfied
Can you feel me
Conceal the
Vice of my heart then
Reveal the
Freedom once the conviction is lifted
So I thank God that I'm gifted
And born again like babies on their second life
Now progress awaits the road.

VOTE
for Stacey Abrams's 2018 Gubernatorial Race

She said when we change Georgia, we change the South
That's the hardest thing that came out of her mouth
They try to paint the picture of an angry black woman
But that's what we need even if they don't want it
Cause please believe they really don't want it
Kemp had the shotgun to remind us we were hunted

But now we are kings and Stacey is a queen
This is what he saw when Martin had his dream
When we change Georgia, we change the South
But if you don't vote, you're just running your mouth
She shows us the picture of a strong proud woman
And that's what we need even if they don't want it
That's exactly where the power is
That's where our finest hour is
They try to scare you with the rhetoric that excites the red base
But their own campaign strategy is blowing up in their face
This is more than a race and it's bigger than race
They try to suppress the vote of the whole human race
And they try to paint a picture of an angry black woman
But that's what we need even if they don't want it
When we change Georgia, we change the south
But if you don't vote you're just running your mouth.

Take a Stand

Asians, Irish, Latinos, and Blacks, Whites
All getting down in the same cipher
Despite the dirty smudges in history
Some people rugged, some refined like calligraphy
Drawn with colorful strokes from colorful folks
The makers of fables, quotes, and old anecdotes
Telling the story of their struggle through the language of their learning
The American Blacks were once hanging, the German Jews were once burning
The Native Americans were once robbed of this land
The once fertile soil in Africa slowly turned into sand

So who has the upper hand in this land where we've all paid
our dues?
But through all the tribulations this chaos continues
Some share conflicting views, some get caught up in politics
Some are out for quick licks, some fall for same tricks
As the clock ticks in this new millennium of information
Secret segregation, a man living on the space station
But this God's creation and we get what He'll give
It's because of Him that those of us who are still alive still live
And there is no sedative that can take away the pain
But there is a potion that we can concoct to help us as a
people gain
Let every human be humane instead of being so greedy and vain
Some are walking around brain-dead, they were mentally slain
By this system that steals from the poor and gives to the rich
We've already recognized that our program has some glitch
But it's quite hard to fix
While it's getting harder to distinguish one from the other,
some caught up in the mix
Of individuality so widespread that being different makes us
the same
We're all characters in a collection of stories, just a different
title and different name
So you read my book and I'll read yours
But when you come to my neighborhood, don't forget to lock
your doors
Because where I'm from, there are some people who rob and
some people who steal
There are some people who fight and some people who kill
Our battle is uphill, but still, we rise
Like the slaves on the Amistad with fire in our eyes
Like the people outside Jericho when the walls came down

Like the people on both sides of Berlin when the walls came
down
Like the victims of Jim Crow when the laws came down
Shhh! Nobody make a sound, I think I hear it coming
Shhh! Tell the drummer boy to start drumming
As a matter of fact, let's start running
Towards salvation and liberation
Because the end is almost here and that's the fall of every nation
And on that day, it won't matter where you're from
Your skin color will be irrelevant on the day He decides to come
From Afghanistan to the United Kingdom
From the Americas to the Caribbean
From Eastern civilization to that of the European
The girl, the boy, the woman, the man
The gays, the Blacks, the anti-Semitic, and the Klan
Because when the situation gets desperate enough, you'll take
your enemy's hand
So let's become one and let's take a stand.

A Thief in the Right

There are these thoughts that I've been dreaming about
That I just can't seem to put into words
But then again
I am a poet
And that is my job
So now I attempt to rob myself of myself only to give it away
Like a thief in the night
Like a thief in the light
I crept into my own windows of the soul
And stole the dream of revolution
I found a new problem packaged with a new solution

And I could not help but grab it
Nab it
And take along with me, this jewel
I mean, I should pocket all that I can
If I didn't, I'd be a fool
Because in this room of ideas
I found in me thoughts that I never knew existed
Or maybe I just couldn't put them into words
It's like trying to fit herds of elephants into small cages
It's like trying to fit wisdom and maturity into a child's early ages
And when I could not put these things onto pages
I thought
I am a poet
And that is my job
So now I attempt to rob myself of my own soul
Only to understand it better and make it more whole
I stole seeds of mass motivation to be planted for the people
I stole strategies and plans formed to make all people equal
And they must be put into effect now because in life there is
no sequel
No chance to come back clean
Only time to redeem our downfalls and strengthen our chain
Yes, these are the thoughts that I borrowed from my brain
These are the things that I stole from my own soul
Like a thief in the night
Like a thief in the light
Creeping out of my own window with bags of insight
With bags of powerful stuff that makes people want to fight
And rise
And rebel
Against this genocide of the mind
A new struggle needing a new movement
Not unlike slavery or civil rights

When we snuck to read books by the light of candle lights
When we rode to freedom on the Underground Railroad
under the canopy of the night
When our houses, hopes, and dreams were riddled with sticks
of dynamite
Thrown by a hand that was white
But now our enemy has a new face
It's a mixed breed, not of any specific race
Sometimes it's black
Sometimes it's invisible which makes it harder for us to chase
But just the fact that I've seen it pushes me to responsibility
And this responsibility I embrace
With open arms
I stole these thoughts from my own treasure box as if they
were trinkets or golden charms
As if I were a thief in the night
A thief in the light
And I know it sounds wrong
But a thief in the right
Like Robin Hood
Never has doing something so bad ever felt this good
Because I'll take these mental riches and distribute them in the
hood
Until crack is no longer the monkey hanging on my brothers' back
Until the pursuit of money and cars no longer leaves my
brothers behind bars
Until the other man can no longer find enjoyment in our
widespread unemployment
Until the majority of the videos stop depicting our sisters as hoes
Until we recognize where the real enemy is and stop treating
our own kind as foes
What happened to unity?
What happened to unity!

What happened to unity?!
Oh, I'll tell you what happened
The government gave us guns and we automatically started clappin'
Then the government gave us drugs and we naturally started trappin'
Just making it easier for the oppressor
Just making it easier for AIDS to kill us when we leave that rubber on the dresser
Just make it easier for the oppressor
So quick to kill another, just because he tried to test ya
So quick to down a brotha every time he tries to bless ya
We'll listen to a pimp before we listen to a professor
My neck or
My back
My Benz or
My 'Lac
Parked in front of my project building filled with roaches and rats
Where is the sense in that?
And it's not just the slum that's the problem because the middle class and aristocrats
Look at the situations and close our eyes and turn our backs
Then sit on our leather sofas and blame it on Republicans and Democrats
But I gotta grab the battle axe
And chop down these trees of shame
And bring pride back to our name
This life is not a game
But if it is, I'll play with precision
And make the right decision
I ask my people to open their eyes and share with me this vision
That I stole from my own soul
To transform my body into a vehicle and let God be in control

And these are the thoughts that I've been dreaming about
That I just couldn't seem to put into words
But then again
I am a poet
And that is my job
So now I attempt to rob myself of myself only to give it away
Like a thief in the night
Like a thief in the light
And I know it sounds wrong
But a thief in the right.

The Potential to Be

What do you have the potential to be?
The P in Penelope?
The wave in the sea?
With the highest crest
Nothing?—No!
Well, maybe yes
But you can't speak life to the negative context
You can't let the unacceptable manifest

What do you have the potential to be?
Everything or nothing at all?
You decide!
And those aren't your only choices
The options are wide
But you must be deliberate in your direction
Wandering just won't do
In order to find your compass
You must first find the God inside you

What do you have the potential to be?
The brightest star in the sky?
The grayest cloud?
The captain of your ship?
The pilot of your craft?
The top pick in the draft?
You decide!
This is no idle task
This is no rhetorical question
You can't just wait on a blessing
Create one!
It is not too late
But you can't worry about the date
And you don't know your fate
But it's you who has to choose
To win or to lose

You decide!
Humble yourself
Escape your pride
Take hold of what you are purposed to be
What do you have the potential to be?

Before I Get Up Out of Here

If you ain't multiplying
You dying
Or standing still
Or tumbling down the hill
But I was taught to persevere
And have no fear
And get what I need from this world

Before I get up out of here

It's a brand-new year
But it could be the last
So my mission is not only to stabilize my future
I'll also rectify my past
I passed through younger years
And it was no crystal stair
But knowledge was embedded into the roots of my hair
My mind and soul are a pair
And my body provides the frame
The characteristics of these three are represented by my name
I'm here to change the game
But it's a brand-new year
And I'll give what I got to this world
Before I get up out of here

Some will aid
Some will oppose
Some will extend a helping hand
Some will turn up their nose
And cover their ears
And follow the ways of their peers
Drowning in ignorance and sinking in tears
While others build towers
And utilize their hours
To combine powers
And these are those who understand my urgency
Holy water is still purging me
While something is urging me to do the right thing
The alarm clock is set, but I don't know when it will ring
I prepare myself now for this brand-new year
So I can get what I need and give

what I got to this world
Before I get up out of here.

The Boundaries of a Book

We no longer have to settle for the seats in the back
Rosa Parks proved that
And it cannot be disputed, this is actual fact
Printed on the pages of history where some of us never look
I once heard the best place to hide the truth is within the
boundaries of a book
Opened by those destined to determine their own tomorrow
Read by those who will learn to lead and learn to follow
And as I write each word that will be engraved onto the pages
And soaked into the pages
I pray that the upliftment will be contagious and affect all ages
Energize the fight through the iniquities to turn them into
victories
Let's avoid the stereotype and create our own identities
We don't have to settle for the seats in the back
It was 1955 when Rosa Parks proved that
And it cannot be disputed, this is actual fact
Printed on the pages of history where some of us never look
I once heard the best place to hide the truth is within the
boundaries of a book.

I am the Total Package

I am the total package
I have everything I need to succeed
This is a game of inches, so I'll give everything I've got

This is a game of adjustments, so I'll be committed but not
stubborn
This is a game of chess, so I'll think three moves ahead
I will focus on where I want to be and not be discouraged by
the challenges along the way
I will not quit
I will not give up
But I will face my fears
And be a leader for my peers
God is on my side, so I cannot lose
When I am weak, He is strong
When I am strong, I remain humble
When I am humble, I do not stumble
And I appreciate the little things
I am equipped with everything I need to succeed
So I am the total package!

BLACK SONGS

I Am Real
for Cornel West & Ralph Ellison

I am real
Tangible
Touchable
Tasteable
Not wasteable
Irreplaceable
With a history almost untraceable
I am real
I have a mind
A beautiful body
A striving soul
Sensibilities
Self-control
Jelly's Last Jam
And a Jelly Roll
Disenfranchised at the poll
But I am real
Yellow sweat stains my white shirts
Blue collars
And black hurts
Soiled struggles
Tainted troubles
Loud yells
And silent cries
Eyes on the prize
Tomorrow never dies
Because I am real
Like a trumpet blast
In classic jazz
A Love Supreme

A deferred dream
A Grand Hustle
An extreme scheme
To get the CREAM
Because baby's gotta eat
And She's Gotta Have It
And these desires are real
This huger is real
These longings are real
Like I am real
Like Bee Bop and Blues
The bad and Good News
These lies made to be trues
Limited choices from which to choose
High cholesterol and AIDS
Sickle cell and diabetes
My face on the box of Wheaties
My mug shot in the paper
Not depicted as the Caped Crusader
A drug dealer
A tax evader
I am real
Something you may hate to feel
But you can feel
You can't deny
I'm "flesh and bone
Fiber and liquids"
Of character and depth
The seventh day He slept
Jesus wept
Moses kept
The commandments for the children of Israel
Out of Egypt

Into the Promised Land
Babylon is rising
New Jerusalem awaits
What if the sign reads "Colored Only" at the Pearly Gates?
Let me in
You see my skin
It represents my pain
They told me brown was a stain
And black was a blemish
But I am real
Respectable
Admirable
Humane
And true
I am real
But I am not like you.

Avarice
for the African People that died in the Transatlantic Slave Trade

Avarice
Sounds like a spell being cast to keep you bound
In the waters of the Atlantic, you drowned
And as I looked into your sinking eyes
I could feel your cries
But I could also feel you rejoicing
Relieved that you won't have to live in the white mans' world
So you mourn for those that made it
Brought halfway around the world only to be degraded
By avarice
Then try to live up to its standards

They gave me whips
They gave me chains
They gave me Christianity
They sold me cars
They sold me clothes
They sold you the sea
And told me I was the one that was free
But you are the lost who are free
From their avarice
As the under currents preserve your soul
And the never-ending tides make sure your story is told
I can see that you haunt them
Every time I look in their eyes
I see through their disguise
I see through their love
I see through their lies
And I see avarice
Like a spell being cast to keep them bound
And we're not supposed to make a sound
Because the more they hear
The more they fear
And wonder how much longer this will be
A white mans' world
Two million souls
That's a lot of sins to make up for
But no matter how much they get they just want more
Because it's avarice
And now
I don't know my name
And my father felt the same
So I'll call myself Garvey
I'll call myself X
I'll call myself King

And I feel you cheering me on
From the surface of the waters and beyond
To go deeper
To go further
To avoid their murder
And live
Bask in the cool waves of your inspiration
And not give in to the sensation
Of their greed.

Papa was a Rolling Stone

Papa was a rolling stone
Wherever he laid his hat was his home
And when he died
All he left us was a loan
An unpaid debt
And the creditors keep on calling
And the predators keep on crawling
And the urban keeps on sprawling
Without us
They doubt us
We doubt us
And underestimate us
Because they played us
And made us
Think they were our forefathers
We are not their sons and daughters
They are ours
So why are we behind bars
Of unlocked cages
Misguided rages

Progressing through these xenophobic stages
Generational phases
Of unawareness and immaturity
And papa
Was a rolling stone
Wherever he laid his hat was his home
And when he died
All he left us
Was alone

But we are not alone
The spirits of our ancestors haunt us
As we squander some of what they bought us
We must remember what they taught us
About how to find our ways back home
And how to pick up the phone
To say I love you
There is nothing above you
And you don't have to prove that
To anyone but yourself
Government assistance cannot subsidize your wealth
And your wealth cannot subsidize your health
Love is not for sale
But it is on the shelf
And window shopping for your soul
Will never make it whole
That requires self-control
So dry your tears
As I wipe my own
Said the fatherless child
Unknowingly sitting on his throne
Thinking papa was a rolling stone
Wherever he laid his hat

Was his home
And we he died
All he left us
Was alone.

We'll All Be One

The rich get richer and the poor get poorer
As another innocent man is sent to prison because of a racist
juror
They say power is in numbers but while we're killing each
other our numbers are growing fewer
My brothers are being drawn to the dope game's hook by its
glamorized lifestyle lure
As the AIDS epidemic spreads throughout the veins of our
youth
Some afraid of getting tested because they can't handle the
truth
And while they were feeding hungry people overseas in
Afghanistan
There were natural American citizens shopping for food in a
garbage can
I saw a homeless man steal with the intensions of getting
caught and going to jail
Because for him, the streets of this crazy world are much
colder than the confines of a cell
He said that life isn't like Heaven on Earth, it's more like living
in Hell
Where everybody has to have something for sale
Be it some useless product or be it your soul
But I've grown tired of this same old system in which I refuse
to grow old

Without making a change and standing up for what's right
I'm not scared to be an individual, I'm not scared of this
world, I won't run from the fight
Not tonight, not ever
Because when it can't get any worse it can only get better
And we've come a long way, but this war isn't over as long as
there are high school dropouts and babies found in dumpsters
As long as this television continues to corrupt the minds of
our youngsters
As long as my brothers are perpetually trapped by parole or
probation
As long as in the rich neighborhood there's happiness but in
the ghetto—mainly frustration
Shame on this nation that tried to put a curse on us
They have the nerve to print on dollar bills "In God we trust"
Well maybe the judge didn't have a dollar in his pocket when
he took that young man's freedom away
Maybe the gangbanger didn't have a dollar in his pocket when
he took another man's life away
But we've got to keep on pushing because this war is not yet won
Unity is in the making and one day we'll all be one.

The Sound I Saw

The sun was shining
The streets were alive and breathing
With the sights and sounds that can sometimes be deceiving
Like when the children sound so happy while they're playing
I saw a homeless man laying on a park bench as if he were
sleep
But I really think he was just praying
Hoping for a better day

While some of the local trap stars took a break from trappin'
to flick the dice against the wall
And as I passed by, I could've sworn I heard them snake-eyes fall
Little Johnny just ran up out the corner store with a pocket
full of stolen candy
Something to drink and a Black & Mild
He's just another wild child forced to live this messed up
lifestyle
But as the sun began to go down
In College Park, Brooklyn, Detroit, Chicago, Houston, LA,
Miami, Bean Town and Orange Mound
The streets all played the same song for my eyes that hear
without flaw
And this is the sound I saw.

Just Gettin' It

I'm just gettin' it
Spittin' it out like facts
Labor breaks backs
It's 2003, and the whip still cracks
While chain gangs mend old railroad tracks
Whose cars once excluded Blacks
Or made them wear slacks and paper hats for 50 cents a day
Just enough pay to make it to the next day
And it's ironic how today we still get treated the same way
But only because we let it happen
Niggas is out here rappin' and trappin'
While these folks are slappin' us in the face
Leaving our tongues with no taste
As we get hypnotized by the treble and the bass
In this rat race

But one day we gotta face the music
It's brains in our heads
One day we gotta use it
Instead of abuse it
Or we all just might lose it
Our elders try to pass down knowledge, but some confuse it
With babble
I dibble-dabble in space-age thoughts
But

I'm just getting' it
Spittin' it out like facts
Labor breaks backs
It's 2003, and the whip still cracks
While most ride the wrong tracks
And brag about whose got the fattest sacks
And multiple hoes in the backs of old school Cadillacs
Minds melting like wax
While the poor pay more tax
And live in shacks or public housing built using bricks
Just another one of the government's tricks
And it's wrong for us to do some of the same things that're
condoned for hillbillies and hicks
While we're out here struggling and dying just trying to get rich
These weak Uncle Tom employees suck supervisor d**ks
Just to keep from being laid off
But I laid off from the fallacies to invest my time in truth
We gotta change the way we raise our youth
It's like they're claustrophobics being born trapped inside a
phone booth
With no quarters to call for help
It hurts me every time I go in-depth
And analyze just how long (as a people) we have slept

And been crept on, stepped on, and left 'lone
But this is deep like baritone
And

I'm just gettin' it
Spittin' it out like facts
Labor breaks backs
Its 2003, and the whip still cracks
And this is like a telegram or fax
To these so-called MC's to tell 'em to stop spittin' lies on
tracks
They got our kids thinkin' it's cool to pack gats
And he's only 16 years old but he already knows how to hit it
from the back
His daddy taught him how to plant the seed
And when the baby comes out, how to not be there when
they're in need
His big brother taught him how to smoke weed
His uncle taught him how to drink
But nobody taught him how to think
So now he's raised up being drained down this socio-political
sink
Made to stop us before we start
Like a body that never pumped blood to the heart
But

I'm just gettin' it
Spittin' it out like facts
Labor breaks backs
It's 2003, and the whip still cracks.

Another Nigga in the Crowd

Can't make own decisions
Can't make my own choices
It doesn't matter how many scream
Because no one hears the voices
Some shout, some whisper, some yell unbearably loud
But no one man is heard
He's just another nigga in the crowd

We all look the same
That's probably what they say
But I consider myself to be different
I walk a separate way
Does my face look like his?
Does his face look like mine?
Anyone who feels that way
Must obviously, be blind
My voice sounds like a murmur
Although I try to be loud
But as long as I'm in here
I'm just another nigga in the crowd

Right foot then the left
On the correct side of the hall
Assume the position, spread the feet
And place both hands on the wall
The name has been replaced
By a number sequence of seven digits
And some of tallest men in here
Begin to act as if they're midgets
But they can't keep me down
Because I choose to live up in a cloud
But for now and only now
I'm just another nigga in the crowd.

Blow

Blow your trumpets fellas
Make the walls come down
I said blow your trumpets fellas
Make the walls come down
Even the haters love your sound

Blow your trumpets fellas
'Til they shut the place down
Blow your trumpets fellas
'Til they shut the place down
But they can't shut down your sound.

Saul-Langston: Bebop Sha Clack Clack
for Saul Williams & Langston Hughes

Saul-Langston is a combination of powers
So immense that it shakes mountains loose
Squeezes fountains for all their juice
And makes the Devil want to call a truce

It sounds like
Bebop
Sha Clack Clack !!

It's the Recitation of Weary Blues
It's the Montage of the Apocalypse
It's the Man Before Before
And the man before him
Letting the pen describe the soul

While painting pictures with typewriters
And using pencils for utensils
The renaissance man of Harlem
The slinger of Amethyst Rocks
Investing in simile stocks
Metaphorical mortgages
And Chocolate Covered Watermelons

It sounds like
Bebop
Sha Clack Clack !!

It's the formula for revolution
Daymares
And Dreams Deferred
Rebirths, Revolts, and Resurrections
It's a dred-head black skinned man from eternity
It's a clean-cut light skinned cat from the times when we were
"colored"
It's a literary genius
Eating alphabet soup
Making fiction real
With supreme diction skill
It's the writer of Ballads
It's the creator of Madam
It's Shakespeare in Harlem
It's Saturn's Rivers flowing through Brooklyn

It sounds like
Bebop
Sha Clack Clack !!

It's World War II

It's a Spirit Growing Seven by Seven
It's the fight against Hitler and Jim Crow
It's 1943
It's 2003
It's a representation of we
Now free
To be
Free
Through pens and papers
They are the shapers
Of mental images
With vivid colors
Like Ruby Brown
And blacks and Blues
Like Red Roses and Indigo On
And the color of invisible
It's the Poet-Trees That Forrest Forever
It's the voice of the ghetto
And

It sounds like
Bebop
Sha Clack Clack !!

A Brown Bag of Miscellany
for Zora Neal Hurston

I am a brown bag of miscellany
Lined up against the wall with other bags—
White, red, and yellow
Turn me upside down
And let my contents be known

Expose my value
Which has no price
Only shape and character
In me you'll find all twenty-seven letters of the alphabet
Waiting to be used
A magnifying glass
A few blue pens (some thirsty for ink)
You'll find a watch that doesn't tell time, but it does tell truth
A roll of quarters
A spool of thread
A fishing hook
A holy book
A box of dreams
And some puzzle pieces
And you stand
Brown bag in hand
Shaking your head
Thinking:
One man's treasure is another man's trash
But who cares what you think?
Get your own bag.

We are President

We are president
We just got elected
We showed up at the polls and we voted for ourselves
In record numbers
We voted for ourselves
When a few years ago—we couldn't even vote for anybody else
Now look at ourselves
They go'n have to put some books up on those history shelves

Because we are president
You know—all that stuff about holding these truths to be self-evident
Has now become more evident
Now that's change that we can believe in
That's hope that we can achieve in
That's a blessing that we barely have room to receive in
And we are president
We are the leader of the free world
Not just talking about the US of A
I'm talking about the world
In a celebratory atmosphere
Praises going up past the stratosphere
Because we are president
We are more than legislation
We are champions of liberation
We are the Dream
American and Black
Black as the oil that flows like red blood
From above the Mason-Dixon down to the red mud
And I am so proud of us
Because we showed up at the polls and we voted for ourselves
And we are president.

Embrace

I am Latin American
Embrace me as I embrace you
As I bring my tempo and flavor to your world of diversity
Give me equality
Prove to me your liberty
I am Puerto Rican

I am Dominican
I am American
Can you accept my history
And make it yours
Will you accept my allegiance and return it with freedom
Why?
Because I am human

I am Asian American
Embrace me as I embrace you
Let my threads contribute to your fabric
Make me feel welcome in your communities
Can we live together in morality under common values
I am Japanese
I am Vietnamese
I am American
Can you respect my traditions
Can you accept change
Can you make the promises this country was founded on a
reality
Why?
Because I am human

I am African American
Embrace me as I embrace you
I am the victim of your past
Let me flourish in your future
Will you try to understand the characteristics of my soul
Prove to me your liberty
I am Kenyan
I am Nigerian
I am American
Can you love me as a brother

Will you water my social seeds
Can you look me in the eyes and see me in equality
Why?
Because I am human

I am Native American
I am Irish American
I am Mexican American
Can you be open to my culture
Will your flag represent my kind
I am your child
I am your youth
Give me a sense of self-worth
Motivate me
Educate me
Clothe me
Embrace me
As I embrace you.

My Mother's Land

They tried to take me from my mother's land
But I'm still there
Somewhere
In the Sahara
Reminiscing on the terror
Which only fuels my fire
Ignited by injustice
Extinguished by victory

They tried to take me from my mother's land
And whip my mind and break my spirits

And deprive me of tomorrow
And they thought they had it made
Until Nat Turner grabbed his blade
And Harriet got on her train
Sweat drips from my brain
Like rain drops from the tree
And they thought they did
But they never knew me
Me being man
With underestimated capabilities
And untapped abilities
Searching for restored tranquilities

They tried to take me from my mother's land
But I'm still there
Fishing from the shores of Madagascar
While peoples racing like NASCAR
Trying to reach the checkered flag
Not knowing that if we would only combine forces
It wouldn't be a race
It would simply be a chase
Trying to catch up with the truth and inspire our youth
But we're so caught up in differences
And building fences
Burning bridges
Falling off cliffs
Lost in valleys
And tripping over rigid ridges

They tried to take me from my mother's land
And they thought they did
But they never knew me
So now I define my identity

With purity once only associated with the color white
I be the night
Bold and cool and dark and lighted by the moon
The sun is my father
And he shines his light over my mother's land from which they
tried to take me
But even the earthquake couldn't shake me
And the Lord wouldn't forsake me
So why do they think they can take me from my mother's
land?
Maybe in body
But not in heart and soul
Zimbabwe is my stomping ground
And I've got cousins near Cape Town
My lineage is of Ethiopian kings who took vacations in Sudan
And bathed their feet in the waters of the Nile
I spoke a thousand languages when I was only a child
Before they tried to take me from my mother's land.

Gunsmoke

So many braindead
Laying dead
Stress heavy like lead
Lies will always be said
While they misled the truth
Mislead our youth
Have 'em thinking they're bulletproof
Or a hundred proof like Golden Grain
Hold inside the pain
99% of this world living in vain
Laying themselves on the track to be run over by the train

Sane or insane
You must maintain
But the main problem runs so deep
That when I lay down, I find it hard to get sleep
But I won't weep
My tears have run dry
I just keep the prize in my eye
But some don't pray until the day that they die
Maybe too late
Why hesitate with God
He's the One that helps you out when easy times get hard
He's the One that will always be able to pull your card
So don't start
Acting as if you got it all under control
He's the One that gives substance to your soul
Ain't nothing new under the sun
It's all old
Let the truth be told
I won't fit into your mold
I won't fold
I spit words that are bold
Cold like the winter
Sometimes it gets hard for me to stay on my agenda
I've never been a pretender
All I know is real
People kill
Rich folks live on a hill
So they don't know how it feels
Down in the trenches
Amongst the rats, roaches, and stenches
Fate clenches the route of us all
But who's go'n still stand tall
Despite it all

There's no cure for this disease
But I'm here to bring the Tylenol
To ease the pain
Put the picture in a frame
Give things with no words a name
Burn the ignorance with a flame
Ignited by my pen
My most powerful weapon
That bangs hard like Lead Zeppelin
I passed most of the testin'
So may the best win
I tend to get deeper than the Pacific
The way I get so specific is terrific
The Lord gave me these skills so I consider myself gifted
Lifted to the next zone
On some other sh*t
Trying to get as much as I can get
But it's not for self
It's for everybody else
At least anyone that's left
After this war
But a lot of us are fighting and don't even know what for
What's the score?
I think I'm winning
But if I'm winning, why is the devil grinning?
As if he has the upper hand
Throughout this land
But God has a plan
And I'll stick to it wherever I stand
Crossing the river or the burning sand
I am the chosen
Frozen to be preserved
Throughout my whole life, I only got what I deserved

I have no fear
I am unnerved
Not deferred, undeterred
From my path
I learned to do the math
When my mind gets dirty, I give it a bath
This stuff ain't funny
My folks are dying over money
Thinking it will save them from their past
But in actuality it's just making their clocks tick too fast
And when they're gone all they can say is that it was all over
cash
But who's go'n last
In the race that doesn't end
Waiting for a second wind
The burst of energy keeps me strong
If this were a battle, I'd still be standing when everyone else is
gone
Once again, I find myself alone
Mind blown by reality
One brother after another becoming a casualty
Gradually we'll see
Eventually we'll be
What God wants us to be
Until then, none of us are free
Just zombies under the spell of society
Obstacles come in a wide variety
No denying me
What lies at the end of the road?
Sometimes I feel like I want to explode
Sometimes when I'm away from home I can't wait to get back
to my pen
So I can slip in

The dimension
That releases my tension
And places my animation in suspension
Who are you?
Who am I?
God's people living under the sky
While Lucifer waits in anticipation for the day he'll see us fry
In eternal damnation
But he's afraid of salvation
Because it decreases Hell's population
Which will be inhabited by souls from every nation
The Puerto Rican and the Haitian
The humans and the spacemen
Pacing back and forth in contemplation
Trying to decide on righteousness or worldly temptation
Prostitution and tax inflation
Free basin'
In this millennium of information
And time wastin'
But I'm facing the truth
And using patience as a virtue
I won't hurt you
And neither will He
We have common goals
But who knows when this will cease?
Who knows when we'll have peace?
Everybody trying to get a piece
Of the pie
Before they die
But why try
If you're not going to hold your head to the sky?
Time goes by
And some don't get the inspiration

The spiritual saturation
The mental penetration
Lacing their blunts with coke
Just something else devilish to smoke
And you say it helps you cope
But how can put your faith in dope?
Now you're up against the rope
So I'm go'n give you words to quote
To heal you like an antidote
And if you still you feel you have to tote
That .38 in your boat
You'll find it to be the reason why your ship won't float
These words can give you life or these words can make you choke
But I'm out like gun smoke.

Unfinished

I'm a mad man
A glad man
A sad man
All wrapped up in one man
Hand me down some knowledge
Hand me down the strength
To go the whole length
Of the field
Of battle where I wield my sword and my shield
While marching up hill
But they can't feel me
Really
I just move like shooting stars
Crossing eight bars

Of insanity like genius
I'm a man from Mars, Jupiter, and Venus
You've never seen this
But I have
I laugh at pity
Which is something that's hard to find in the city
Of red clay
And black top
Brown boy
And white cop
Stop to witness the execution of liberty
Carried out by the henchmen of greed
Plant me like a seed
And watch something new take form
Solo like the horn on a unicorn
Born in the black
Stabbed in the back
Trained to attack
And hack away
At the troubles of the day
Who's to say what's right
I make my own opinion for which I fight
In the middle of the moonlit night
While I sat at a 3-legged 4-cornered table
And used my mind to keep it stable
Able to support frustration then make it disintegrate
Integrate tradition and change
Even though it sounds strange and out of range
But the tides brought in new life
Isaac was willing to make the sacrifice with a knife
Profound in thought
Lucid with depth
Vivid with sound and light and color

Over land I hover like a helicopter chopper
Pop and locker
I'm the door knocker, let me in
So I can see what lies on the other side
Society has something to hide from me...

REVERSE ENGINEERING MY DREAM

The Man I'm Supposed to Be

Looking at myself
And asking what I see
The man I am today
Or the man I'm supposed to be
And who is he to me
Exercising equilibrium and buoyancy
New levels of loyalty
No need for any endorsing me
Divorcing the very idea of normalcy
Something truer is taking form in me
Learning politics and diplomacy
Sometimes it's just ol' lonely me
Motivated by the blessing that there is only one of me
Which doesn't make me irreplaceable
There's always someone out there more capable
God's will is what preauthorizes my success
And drives me to be the best
Regardless of the region
I must always pass His test
Which requires the introspection of my decisions and my direction
Analysis of my predilection
And usage of protection
From all the trappings and innerworkings of the things that would celebrate my destruction
And hamper my production
Taking into consideration all the sources of instruction
Because I'm not a very good soldier
But a warrior indeed

Even the general is somewhat limited by what comes with
rank and prestige
But I feel like I'm in the Negro League
Traveling over the seas and under the breeze
On a mission to supply what's currently in need
And has always been in need
Of fulfilling
Only warranted for the willing
Blood spilling
Has occurred on the field of battle for the spirit and the mind
But the day comes when we all have to fight—this just
happens to be mine
It's not for you, this is for me
And prerequisite for the fulfillment of my divine destiny
Which is not just for me
And way bigger than me
I'm not at the center
I'm a king but the King of kings is Who allows me to enter
So I humble myself like a mentee to a mentor
Stepping back to look at myself
And asking what I see
The man I am today
Or the man I'm supposed to be.

Improving as a Person

Your life improving over time
Can be a sign of you improving as a person
The constant desire to be better
Paired with the appropriate actions can create measurable results
Or immeasurable results!
Self-discipline

Self-improvement
Self-motivation
Will all be required at times
There might not always be a shoulder to lean on
And even those that are in your corner are imperfect
As we all are
But we all are in some way accountable to our purpose
How well do we take it into account?
Are we giving our full amount?
And your life improving over time
Should be a sign of you improving as a person
Your family benefits
Your community gains value
And you are better positioned than you were when they saw
you the last time
Because you have been committed to constantly changing for
the better
Through the growth
And no matter what's going on around you
Who you are on the inside is going to matter
How well do you know your self?
The better you understand your weaknesses and strengths
The better equipped you are to succeed
Are you driven?
If so, what drives you?
What angers you? and why?
When are you at your best?
Or worst?
How much time do you spend somewhere in between?
The answers can be applied to improvement
As you pursue your goals and dreams
And your life improving over time
Can be a sign of you improving as a person.

Dream

Dream in vivid color
Dream in HD
Dream in 3D
Dream me
Dream I in a different context
Dream in what's next
Dream in something you can see
Dream of something you can be
And make that your goal

And make that your goal
Dream of something you can be
Dream in something you can see
Dream in what's next
Dream I in a different context
Dream me
Dream in 3D
Dream in HD
Dream in vivid color.

What is Motivation for the Masses?

Experiences translate to wisdom
when we learn from them
It feels good to go through those experiences
And gain that wisdom
To share with someone else
To either uplift them
Or warn them

Or inspire them
And that's what motivation for the masses is
Me sharing my story as it unfolds
Leaving me vulnerable and exposed
And subject to yes's and no's
That were unpredictable
But ultimately guiding me to a place of elevation
And major victories in spite of minor defeats
It is my purpose
Of which I'm so appreciative to have and know
Because for so many, it is not so
It's beyond valuable whether you have it or not
But in all thy getting
Get understanding
Knowing your purpose is knowing your worth
Knowing your worth is knowing your place
And if your place is amongst the kings and queens
There's nothing else that can replace fulfillment
God made you
So your success is in His interest
He wants you to win
And so do I
That's what Motivation for the Masses is
Sharing my learning through sharing my life
In the tradition of my ancestors
By writing it down like hieroglyphics on the walls of ancient
tombs
And now I'm learning how to see a finished picture
To make the yes's and no's more predictable
Applying the wisdom that came from the experiences
That came from that time when I had to fight
Or that time when I had to push
Or that time when I had to fall back

Or that time when I had to grow
And that's what motivation for the masses is
Living my life as an example
As imperfect and empowering as it may be
To the reader
And the naked eye
Or the enlightened folks
I'm just learning to master destiny
And be what I'm destined to be instead of all the other options
That's what Motivation for the Masses is.

One Step at a Time

Part I

One step at a time
I diversify my mind and variate my rhyme
With steady inclines
Searching for signs
And new designs for the future
New designs for the now
And forever
Whether day or night
One step at a time
I diversify my mind and variate my rhyme
Sometimes just to burn time
With production
Trying hard as I can not to be distracted by seduction
While maintaining movement
Mental movement being manifested in the form of the
physical
My thought patterns are lyrical

But the mental and the physical
Won't survive without the spiritual
So when I close my eyes I pray just to keep the connection strong
'Cause at times He was the only One that kept me holding on
Knowledge is long
And unlimited
So I diversify my mind and variate my rhyme
I'm glad it's not a crime
'Cause I'd be somewhere locked up every time the light shines on my mind.

Part II

Freedom is a blessing
Yet so taken for granted
Something that has to be taken
Because nobody will grant it
Eyes slanted no longer against the grain
I move with the breeze
But stay strong like steel chains
While eating good food for the brains
Getting wiser with the grind
I diversify my mind and variate my rhyme
One step at a time
I'm trying to reach that prime
That doesn't exist
This is endless
Yet I persist.

Back to the Basics

Back to the basics
Face it
Embrace it
Don't chase it
Don't waste it
Instead take it
To the next level
Then look back at what you started with
And made something out of whatever it was
And not just because
Being driven by Love
That means there is a Purpose
Beneath your surface
Or above your surface
At no point in your life were you ever worthless
Even if they made you feel that way
But you build that way
Much stronger than the average
In spite of all the damage
Sustained over the years
Back to the basics
Face it
Embrace it
Don't chase it
Don't waste it
Instead take it
To the next level
Then look back at what you started with.

Temptation

Leadeth me not into temptation
Temptation is the antagonist of my focus
My focus is the antagonist of my temptation
They are forever enemies
And I've got too much to lose
If temptation is what I choose.

What's the Point?

What's the point in having a grand dream
If you never make it real
What's the point in having an ultimate goal
If you never achieve it
In standing near the floor
But you never dance
In blaming circumstance
What's the point in never being satisfied
If you're never being satisfied
Why not just be content in your lament
Why aim high
If you're not going to pull the trigger
Why dream bigger
If you're going to think small
Wouldn't it be easier to not dream at all
At least you wouldn't be up at night
In the idle man's plight
Thinking of what you would do
Or should do
Only to get up and not get it done

That anguish weighs a ton
And carrying it is no fun
If you're going to wait for your shot
Then someone else may as well shoot
Since you're not going to execute
What's the point
You're doing yourself a disservice
To not try because you're nervous
Or calculated risk averse
Why train in short bursts
For the marathon
Why set yourself up to lose
And blame others for what you choose
You'll drive yourself mad
Harping on what you never had
There is nothing that you cannot do
When you're willing to do
Whatever it takes
Even if it means swimming across lakes
Or playing games of high stakes
Or persevering through bone breaks
And let downs
Setbacks and self-inflicted wounds
Your mettle will be tested
But your sweat is well invested
When invested in your dream
But what's the point
If you never make it real
Or give up when it's uphill
Why aspire to the top
If you're going to stop
What's the point?

Volume 4

Right now, I'm living volume 4
In real time
So I try my best not to spill time
I still grind
And my purpose has not changed
Motivation for the Masses is synonymous with my name
Digging deeper into consciousness
As I progress through every step
Even though I have been wounded
And each time fine tuned it
Living my life right now, I have to be better than before
I refuse to make a sad story out of volume 4
Walking through a door of opportunity
But not impunity so principles are required
If you're going to be admired
By anybody looking at you hoping to be inspired
And right now, it's more important than it ever has been
before
For me to stick to the values that are embedded into my core
Especially in volume 4
The newscasts predict brighter weather
And plans are slowly coming together
That's the spice of life
Not a roll of dice
Amazing in the picture
And now it's easier to focus
And avoid all the locusts
Blessed and highly favored moving past the cliché
Working to strengthen my Relationship everyday
Giving what I can but need to give a lot more
While I'm living volume 4.

Queen Back

I just got my Queen back
And the only way to get a queen back
Is to push a pawn to the edge of the other side
And the queen is the most valuable piece
Aside from the ultimate win or loss
I'm stronger with my Queen
My strategy has been made more keen
But she was lost
The greatest blow I've taken in this battle
And the reaction to my action hadn't started off too well
It seemed like a good move at the time
But hindsight is closer to 20/20

An angel confided in me and recommended I get my Queen
back
Even if the bishops fall
Sacrifice is required wherever there is greatness
Humility is an asset as I exercise patience
And it's harder to win without my Queen
Balance at the decision making level thrives on the foundation
Who will defend your flanks?
And to get that pawn to the other side is a feat within itself
It necessitates a lot of focus to maneuver forward
Without getting separated from the true objective
To obtain victory in every battle that is worth picking
Or one that is not of your choosing
But I counterattack
By getting my Queen back.

So Far

We've come so far together but I've got so far to go
There are things I've yet to go through but You already know
I've been through peaks and valleys but have not yet seen the top
You remind me that I will get there if I keep faith and refuse to stop
The cards may be stacked against me, but You are stacked against the cards
Your provision was established before me, before my journey even starts
But I have to be bold and courageous and look adversity in the eye
There are so many excuses that could be made—so many reasons not to try
But in You there is only victory when paired with the will to win
You put purpose in all existence and reveal it to the hearts of men
You reveal Your truth to me though there are many things I do not know
We've come so far together but I've got so far to go.

Downloading...

I was browsing on the world wide web and found exactly what
I was looking for on one of those peer-to-peer networks
I had to search through the meaningless
The perverted exploits
The attractive distractions
But ultimately, I found exactly what I was looking for
It was a rather large file
Of which, not many were indulging

So I knew it would take all night
However, my excitement was not stymied
With a left-click, I was on my way
But initially, it had trouble connecting
And I had to tweak settings before it would queue
But when it finally started
It picked up momentum
Much to my felicitous delight
My optimism was kindled
As I watched the speed rise like me in the morning
So I left it there for other pursuits
Knowing its progress was residual
I washed some clothes and read a book
As the download slipped to back of my mind
But as chapter eleven came to a close
I glanced at the computer screen
To find out just how far it had come
It had only accomplished three percent
Disappointment stained my mood
I watched impatiently as it dragged along
It was getting nowhere fast
But there was nothing I could do
So I went to sleep and woke up the next day
Assuming it would be done
Twelve percent greeted me with a yarn
And I thought I might give up
Abandon it completely
But then it accelerated
So I kept on
And decided to see it through
But to this day
I am still
Downloading my dream.

When You Find That Vision

When you find that vision
Survive the inquisition
And still maintain your balance and stay on the mission
Focus is a standard
Principles are key
Purpose finds definition—making it clearer to see
It is possible to be...
What you were created to be
But you have to want it
And you have to own it
Hold yourself accountable to your success
There are others that have won with much less
Or much more
We are all equivalent at our core
That's the part they've tried for years to get you to ignore
But you have Purpose
Even when you thought you didn't
When you didn't feel the change and you felt like quitting
Keep fighting
For what you know is right for you
To the victor the reward is rightly due
Make your decision
When you find that vision.

Excuses Don't Apply

And this is the start of a new chapter
With too many tools to let failure be an option
Excuses don't apply
And I have to be able to look you in the eye

With every setback and every success
And say I put forth my full effort even when it looks effortless
Or like it's about to make me stop
But you support me by my shoulders on this trek up to the
top
And relieve me of my stress
With every setback and every success
I have to be able to look you in the eye
Because excuses don't apply.

Beyond the Foundation

This is beyond the foundation
Elevation
Another level
Of battling the devil
Of pedal to the metal
Of learning and earning
This is beyond the foundation
That has already been laid
By the soldiers before us who braved
Circumstances that required improvement
Like ours today
And they made a way
For us to build past the foundation
And go beyond
And individually I have been the victim of my own limitations
Until I realized they are not limitations
They are factors in these equations
And I must find a way to win
Utilize chess moves for the master men
Deliberately embody the balanced master blend

To build on what you've been through
To another level
Elevation
Beyond the foundation.

Blessings & Mistakes

Appreciate your blessings
Learn from your mistakes
And use that to survive the high stakes and bad breaks
Stand out and blend in like a Brazilian chameleon
If that's what you have to do rise
But never let go of the real reason you strive
The world is going to take its dips and dives
So hedge yourself against uncertainty
Dream your dream and strategize
And appreciate your blessings
'Cause where would you be without them?
That's why I remain grateful
Even in a world where there are so many around us that are
hateful
So learn from your mistakes
And use that to survive the high stakes and bad breaks
And there will be some
But what would you do differently if you could look back like
a rerun?
Now therein lies the lesson
As you learn from your mistakes
And appreciate your blessings.

My Passion

You gotta be a geek about something
You gotta be passionate about something
My passion is motivation
I don't want to motivate people to think I'm great
I want my greatness to motivate people to know that they are
also great
My best leadership is my example
I want the way I live my life
To have a positive impact on the way that others live theirs
Not so I can make any claim on someone else's success
But so I can live out my passion
That God gave me
And anointed me with
I'm entrusted with purpose just like everyone else
But not like anyone else
If that makes sense
To you.

I Have Taken My Losses

I have taken my losses
And many of them were self-imposed
Maybe all of them were self-imposed
But they were replaced with goals
And the goals were instituted via dreams
Higher things
Meant for kings
Meant for me
And the purpose that I serve
Yes—I have taken my losses

But now is the time for restoration
And replenishment
And refocus
A doubling down so to speak
A strengthening of what was weak
More productivity in every week
Vision where I was blind and distracted
Detracted
By the times that I reacted but should have proacted
And gotten ahead of the curve

And I have taken my losses
I knew that I would have to rebuild
And make it count
And now is the time for restoration
Reinstatement of my reverse engineered dream
Motivation for the Masses is the recurring theme
In the higher things
Meant for kings
Meant for me.

The Brink of a Breakthrough Pt. II

I stand on the brink of a breakthrough
Have you ever been in an unstable place yet standing strong
and confident because you trust God and your readiness for
the place that He is about to take you
When the most important things are staying diligent and
faithful
Appreciative and grateful
No longer bogged down by the petty things

Accepting the role of royalty, walking amongst those that are
already kings
And I am what love made me—capable and accountable
And I am a fish in the water—at my best and undrownable
The doubt has been silent and the hate under the surface
Yet ultimately ineffective as I move forward in my purpose

And now I stand on the brink of a breakthrough
Not deterred by the tides that I must wade through
I've been tested but I stayed true
I've been living by Palms chapter 1 and Romans chapter 8
Staying humble in the process of embracing the understanding
that I was made to be great
I'm the master of my fate because I know God
No fear in my eyes so when I look in the mirror is when I
show God
That I know how to go hard
Because He taught me to go hard
And I stand on the brink of a breakthrough
Living life on a whole new level but the next level already has
a date due
With a new and improved order of operations
Momentum and motivations
Nosebleed elevations
The ability to do more good and a desire to match
I know how to get fire from the match
Before I was just strong, so it was easy to see my muscle
Now I'm more than that and it's easy to see I have hustle
And the seasons that are ahead are more fruitful than those
that are behind
And it's not just all in my mind
I recognize the time
When it's time for me to be the sun and shine

While staying diligent and faithful and appreciative and
grateful
As I stand on the brink of a breakthrough.

Untitled

I fall down and step up at paces that save faces without sparing
my own
My sharing is known
My daring has grown
To the peril of adversarial elements
That tried to set my precedents but couldn't hold me
I refuse to let my failures mold me
He who angers me controls me, so I keep a cool head
They prodded me to no reaction
Made them think I was dead
But I wasn't
I was rising
From beneath the surface
My submersion was worth it as much as it hurted
With disaster I flirted but did not wed
I kicked her out of my bed when I was done
One day I'll say I won
One day I'll say I won.

You Can't Stop Me

You couldn't stop me if you tried
Yes, some have tried
But that time comes when we all have to decide
That we won't let our dreams be pushed to the side

Sticks & stones could break my bones but words will never
leave me teary-eyed
Because I've already cried
Died and came back to fulfill this mission
Now I do more praying than wishing
In a lake of love—I'm fishing
The blue sky—I'm kissing
I'm so glad I've learned to listen
With my ear to the streets
Bobbing my head to the raindrops' beats
That pound on the pavement of the ghetto, the blocks, the
hood
So misunderstood
By those on the outside looking in
Every now and again they drive through just to say that they've
been
When they go home to their land of puffy pillows and pussy
willows
Stray bullets shatter insecure windows
Now I doze into a deep sleep
Having a dream seeing a time when tech-9's and streetsweepers
no longer streetsweep
And the geekers no longer have to creep
In the alleys of the night
Where a lighter flame is the only light
And it shines so bright
But they still walk around blindly
Long ago they lost sight
Most lost the will to fight
Hold on, my dream just went wrong although it started off right
I'm here to be a part of the solution instead of being a part of
the problem

It seems like there's more problems than there are people
trying sincerely to solve them

But you couldn't stop me if you tried
And don't try to use my troublesome past against me because I
have nothing to hide
I'm proud of myself, but I won't get lost in pride
I glide on another level
I'm a soldier—the Lord put me here to march against the devil
And several have tried but they can't stop me
I'm going to get to my destination
You can count on that like that old jalopy that always got you
there on time
Thank God for the little things
Like the scent the kitchen brings
To my nose on Thanksgiving
Or the countless times I woke up with oxygen in my lungs
happy to be still living
Or just understanding the fact that receiving is not as good as
giving
Keep ya head up! to my niggas that make up 60% of the
population in prison
It's a cruel system so let's avoid the trap
You're better off getting an education or trying to rap
The penitentiary is full of brothas that thought they had to
gun clap
It's time to tap into our blessings and begin to nurture our
fruits of the spirit
And I know you hate to hear it
But doing wrong will only take you so far
You better find out who you are
And stop doing the same ol' same ol'

'Cause they can't stop me if they tried
I've already died and came back to fulfill this mission
Of dishing out the truth until y'all cups runneth over
And until y'all cups runneth over
It ain't over
I'm taking this from November to October
Now try to stop me
And watch how fast I drop the
Burden and then flip it around and use it to my advantage
Watch how fast I drop the
Burden then flip it around and use it to my advantage
"I will not lose" is what I chanted
Nothing of this world has power over me
A million haters combined in one line coming one at a time
couldn't stop me from being me
Whether I'm broke or getting money longer than Peachtree
So, hey world—prepare yourself because I'm coming
With truth bitter
You can keep the glitter
And this is truly genuine, so I don't care if you try to copy
Just as long as you realize that you can't stop me.

19 CHRONICLES

May 11th: 2020

15 turns to zero and zero turns into a million
Men, women, and children
This is an uncomfortable feeling
But I still have to find the ceiling
God willing.

December 3rd: 2020

Georgia is at the center
Of a battle between republican and democrat
At the center of this universe of political theater
It's funny how they draw the lines
Between people
Even though we're living together
But living apart
Separated from each other's trues
The red pills or the blues
The haves and the have nots
This election cycle has shown us how important our votes
really are
And every vote really is
The right has been bled for
And Atlanta is at the center.

May 21st: 2020

I'm proud of my people
I see us interacting in positive ways

Interconnected by radio waves and fiber-optic highways
Creating bridges to our selves and to our futures
Indeed brighter
If we make the conscientious effort to conceive it
And many won't achieve it
These are perilous times
Too heavy for petty crimes yet preempting petty crimes
And major ones
Against our ability to recover
We have to find and use the hidden tools and implement them
to uncover
The opportunity
To accelerate growth
I'm proud of my people
Who deal with negative impact and positive both
Playing it smart while setting new goals
And connecting over cyber roads
And I see us.

May 28th: 2020

How many
Black men
Have to be murdered
Unjustly
At the hands of white police
In this country
Before chaos erupts
And spreads like a virus?

June 5th: 2020

I was in a zone on my phone
Getting caught up on what's been going on
Hearing different perspectives within and without our
community
We were right in the middle of a negative that could be turned
into opportunity
And then this jumps off
Another once in 50 years situation
That interrupts our nation
And beyond with globalization
The whole world feels like it's on our side and against us
It's easier to identify who's not really with us
And as I scroll, I see a lot of what I'm not used to seeing—
reality
What's being pushed on social platforms has been a raw truth
about what's happening
In our country
Like I've never seen before
And that's a good thing
As horrific and disturbing as the content is
Because what it was before was lie after lie
A rabbit hole full of ignorance and targeted marketing
Data harvesting and mind boggling misinfluence
With all of us having ready access
5G for the planet
As I was in a zone on my phone
Getting caught up on what's been going on
And what I'm finding is so informative
The jargon is still out there
But the positivity has increased

While simultaneously emboldening hate speech
I saw Barack give us wisdom
I saw people sacrificing fear in order to protest
And capture it all on social media
So no one can deny what really happened
The hate and the attacking
The love and the confusion
All seen through a face mask
But finally revealed from behind the mask
Of filters and photoshopping
And propping oneself up.

May 17th: 2020

Being able to spend this kind of time with you has been
remarkably beneficial
It has allowed me to see our relationship from another perspective
To see you from a different space
I've had the privilege of better understanding your aura
It all connects from your mind and body and soul
How you consume
How you create
How you curate your influence on our experience together
You don't follow a written recipe but you know what to put in it
Yet you're open to new ingredients that pass the taste test
And I love that
About you
This time has revealed even more of your beauty to me
Now I'm appreciative to a higher degree
Because of what I've learned about you.

March 26th: 2020

It's interesting how
When you see people close to each other in public
It's a sign that they really love each other
No gatherings of more than 10 people
And avoid physical contact
In an effort to combat
The coronavirus.

April 26th: 2020

This has that perfect balance
The perfect storm
The world deformed
But not indefinitely torn
From its potential
And there is mourning
And sojourning
Nowhere near defeat
Though it can feel that way
We heal that way
And come together
Like flesh beneath stitches
Like the truth from statistics
This is an opportunity
As opportunistic as that may sound
Either way, stand your ground
In this cyclical economy
Numerical like Deuteronomy
And the S&P 500
Either over or under it

You run with it
Make up your mind
That this is your time.

June 30th: 2020

We all have a part to play in protest
What is mine?
Do I stand in line to cast my vote
Or put words together that instill hope?
God, help me to make a difference
Because the one thing the world has no place for right now—
is indifference
America is more polarized in 2020 vision than I've ever seen it
You're either for us or against us
Because Black Lives Matter
And the enemy shall scatter
And we all have a part to play in protest
But what is mine?
I can't find peace of mind
Because my effortlessness has been replaced with restlessness
Tossing and turning in my dreams
I can't breathe through choke-held screams in Instagram streams
What does the movement need from me?
Contributions to blue campaign candidacy?
Defund the police and have lawlessness in the streets?
Maybe the cops should have to live on the blocks they walk
the beats
If my brother is attacked by 12 and I intervene
Will that result in us both being murdered onscreen
In HD
Fear is the only reason I can think of that they have to hate me

The façade of "white superiority" has always been at its core—
insecurity
So afraid of not having power
That they resort to tactics of divide and devour
But these are the final hours
And we all have a part to play in protest
What is mine? What is yours? What is ours?
The only force that defeats hate is love
So we have to love each other like we haven't in a long time
We can do it because we come from a long line
Of powerful predecessors who passionately persevered to make
Our Lives great again
I come from a king bloodline that got severed in time
Let's reconnect with our ancient history
Our story wasn't always tainted with misery
We built pyramids, created mathematics and language, and
laid the foundations of human civilization
In comparison, America doesn't even come close to being the
greatest nation
From black to white to native American to straight to queer to
however else we want to label each other and define
We all have a part to play in protest
But what is mine?

August 28th: 2020

I heard a concerto on the white house lawn
We used to work from dusk 'til dawn
On this bloodied land we're standing on
The truth about these old bones is painted in all kinds of
colors
But not like Picasso, Banksy, or Leonardo

More Romare than you dare
To acknowledge the tragedies that we breathe through masks
of passionate ignorance
Insignificance
Blatant maleficents
Being sang on the white house lawn
In the background one thousand more soles are passing on
Through plasma-coated dreams
Lab-tested schemes
And vaccinated themes
That don't even protect us from the first strain
You are the beginning and the end
I'll confess this while I'm praying
We've withstood the worst pain
As commonly as a mothers' birth pain
But in a form that they will never know
Though empathy may grow
And enable a renewed path to understanding
As harmonious as the voices beyond the gates
That chant against your hates
From the white house lawn
With spectacles of clarity, confidence, and confederacy
Living up to the legacy
Of Jim Crow and General Lee
Lincoln and John F. Kennedy
And Rockefeller records
As another one of us bites the dust
Only to rise like the Phoenix
While they were distracted by the fires
And misled by the liars
And enchanted by the choirs
That performed a concerto
On the white house lawn.

May 10th: 2020

What if I could write an app that could solve all your
problems
Just type them into the search engine, charge up, and watch it
solve them
Any issues you can think of: finances, loneliness, whatever
It uses the information in your profile to piece your life back
together
It learns your social tendency and true sexual identity
Every vulnerability and emotional dependency
Would you pay me for the privilege of collecting your search
history
If I told you that in doing so, it can alleviate your misery
Make you feel the way you've always wished you felt
Filter out your debt and replace it with secured wealth
Get your brother out of prison or help you navigate the deal
Or is this app
Already real?

August 23rd: 2020

Black Brown
Black smile
Black frown
You can't hold Black down
Even though Black drowned
In the lake of hate that feels more like an ocean
Suppression and soul
Black diamonds Black gold
You would be mortified by the stories Black told

Always the underdog
In a fight that never seems to end
And the only ones who've seen the end
Are the ones who've already seen their end
Where did Black even begin
Before God created light, there was Blackness
It represents the unknown
But what it represents is so strong
I'm Black
As the night or at least a warm dawn
And proud
Black swan
Black pawn
Black king
Unidentified in the roses
But at home in luxury
Menhotep-style
Across the Nile as it flows towards the moon
We shine our brightest at noon
We are the sun gunned down too soon
Bold and beautiful
And you can't hold Black down
Black frown
Black smile
Black Brown.

May 10th: 2020

I remember when Spring meant girls in rompers
But I saw cars lined up for food backed bumper to bumpers
CNN runnin' their cycle
It's easy to find information amongst sources that think like you

I just caught VICE on Showtime
I sit on my balcony and read Bloomberg when I'm on my
slow-grind
Still wasting no time
Earbuds bumping that book I downloaded on Audible
1.5 times faster than real-time
Wash my hands twice before mealtime
He said Clorox might be the cure
This is what we must endure?
Misinformation makes it hard to trust you people
A culture of hate emboldened for a sequel
Led by one with no ability to relate to the struggles of real
people
As Fox 5 gives me the updates
And I eat from home-cooked dinner plates and higher stakes
100 push-ups when I wake and get in some stomach crunches
The invisible enemy holds no punches
I take my daily Bible dosage
Keeps me clean like organic apple cider vinegar
Burns like corrosive
As I switch to channel 46
After which get booed up with Netflix
And chill.

May 29th: 2020

I see my people
In many cases misrepresenting themselves
Digitally connected and extremely effective
But are we considering what's affected
By what we present to this pandemic world
From the streets to the virtual college campuses

And I am not a circumstantialist
I am an optimist
We Will Get Past This
But what we do now dictates what that looks like
I see my people
Turn this negative into a positive
Building up your knowledges
Not bolstering the derogative
Or misnomering ourselves
Striving for whatever they're providing
Like bait on a hook
I see my people
Evolving
Identifying problems and solving
From Ghana to the U.K.
To LA to the pavement I run on every day.

September 30th: 2020

Why are you so mad?
Why are you so angry?
Black people kill each other all the time
Why is it appalling to see one more dying?
Why are you disturbed?
Why do you protest?
Why is there civil unrest?
This is not America at her best
We freed you
We let you vote
For you, we amended our beloved Constitution
We used elegant legislation to implement a solution
We fought a civil war to release you from slavery

And those who fought to keep you in chains, we celebrate for
their valiance and bravery
Why do you want to see their monuments fall?
Instead of gallantly standing tall over you all
Do you really believe racism is systemic?
Or is that just your sad excuse, your hoax, or your gimmick?
Don't take this the wrong way
Don't take these words as weapons
I genuinely wish to understand
Can you answer for me these questions?

Why am I so angry?
Why am I so mad?
This pain is deeper than you know but you tell me it's not that
bad
Yes, it's true that America is the greatest country on this earth
But she was formed in the inequality that she has carried since
her birth
Being born brown automatically comes with a unique set of
challenges
Whether or not you agree
And if you don't, you're either blinded by denial, privilege, or
guilt
Either way, you cannot see
What are the inherent obstacles levied against one simply
because they were born white?
What terrible force has ever perpetrated your plight?
I'm not trying to drive a wedge between us or reverse the
progress of race relations
I'm trying to help you understand why we express these great
frustrations
These burning sensations that we never asked for or deserved

The oppression that we have endured, you have only had to observe
You honestly can't see the parallels between the slave catchers and racist police
Who hunted and harassed us through the fields and forests now the same thing in the streets
For four hundred years you taught us to love, fear, and depend on our white masters
And you conditioned us to hate each other
And you wonder why so many of our households have fatherless children and single mothers
For four hundred years our men were emasculated and prevented from protecting their wives
Many of whom were raped and had their babies torn from their arms with tears in their eyes
We were pitted against each other from the big house to the field
From those with black skin against the fairer skin
These are scars we're still trying to heal
For four hundred years this went on and was proceeded by sharecropping and Jim Crow
And even after desegregation and northern migration we were confined to the harsh conditions of the ghetto
Yes, some of us have matriculated into some of the highest rungs of society
But as whole, we still feel the residues of oppression, suppression, and anxiety
With every generation our fortunes have gotten incrementally better
But the struggle for equality is nowhere near complete
Racism is holding on for dear life but has not yet suffered ultimate defeat

Instead of being so brazen and blatant (for survival) it has had to become more discrete

That's why "Make America Great Again" sounds to many of us like the revival of hate-speak

Because there has not been a time in the history of this great nation where the blacks' burden has been completely natural

We make up maybe thirteen percent of the free the population but over fifty percent of the incarcerated

These numbers are real and factual

We are disproportionately affected by just about everything

From disease and healthcare, to poverty and education, to gentrification and even the coronavirus

So I appreciate the voices that have refused to remain in silence

There have always been those of you that have stood with us against injustice

Who battled alongside us through this country's struggles

From abolition and wars to marches and freedom rides on busses

Who have abided by the biding of the love coursing through their veins

Who know that we are all in this together and when we bleed, we bleed the same

That there is oxygen in our lungs and the same salt in our sweat and tears

That there are enemies foreign and domestic that wish to see us realize our fears

And every time they attack, we rush to each other's aid

We're all dealing with the sins and triumphs of our fathers and sleeping in the bed they made

I appreciate the sentiment of those who genuinely wish to understand

And am humbled when I come across one willing to extend a helping hand
This problem is more complex than trigonometry, but I've tried to explain it as simply as I can
There is no respectable reason why we should not be united across this land
So, let us American Exceptionalists be the example of the power of the collective
Through the edification of our brotherhood and the sharing our perspective
Because until we look beneath the surface, all we see is each other's reflections
And I hope that maybe a little, I've been able to answer for you these questions.

November 6th: 2020

We saw Atlanta change
While we stayed true to its ideals
Keep it real is in our steel
Imported from all around the world
The transplant city
Curated with the best from around the country
And around the globe
Where you from?
No matter where
If you've been living here for years
You're one of us
If you stayed true to its ideals
We saw Atlanta change
But over time, it changed for the better
We are connected to the legacy of Dr. Martin and Coretta

And that lives on
As hazy as it sometimes seems
Amongst the politics and violent scenes
What happened to the dream?
It got reimagined

We saw Atlanta change
We lost John Lewis and CT Vivian on the same day
And they gained immortality
To live on as kings and represent Atlanta
In the archives of our history
I love this city
From College Park to East Point
From Northside to Memorial Drive
From Ponce de Leon
To the West End on the West Side
From Dunwoody to Stone Mountain

We saw Atlanta change
As we shifted to make room for the world
The Hollywood of the South and a tech boom
Rezoning and gentrification
It wasn't comfortable for us all
Because a voucher only goes so far
We became the Blue Star of the South
Rising beyond our surroundings
As the Terminus of talent
With keep it real in our steel
While staying true to its ideals
We saw Atlanta change.

December 24th: 2020

They found the cure real quick
And I didn't even feel sick
But the whole world's gone insane
So they wanna vaccinate my pain
The shot is free but they sold me lies
I invested in Moderna and watched the market reach record highs
While morale reached a record low
Americans are so polarized in a time where patriotism is supposed to grow
A common enemy like the common cold
Unless you've got an underlying condition or you're getting old
You can wait on a stimulus check
And stay away from public train and plane
But the real kicker comes when they try to vaccinate your pain
You can't pick the needle or the vein
Not even the brand name
Is Phizer wiser?
Should China pay the price?
Should we stay away from our families this Christmas to celebrate Jesus Christ?
It's a Covid world we're living in
And it's making some of us stronger
Yet, so many people are hurting and can't keep holding on much longer
As livelihoods crumble under the weight of economic and emotional strain
They won't eradicate the disease, but they'll vaccinate my pain.

June 3rd: 2020

How much hate does one have to be mad
When a man hears the anthem and kneels
But feel nothing when a man kneels
On the neck of an unarmed individual
Relentlessly
Without even yielding when the life leaves the man?
Hate is a disease for which we've never seemed to cure
Even though we know the cure
Is love.

How much more of this can one take
When the silence finds the break
After seeing one's brother being treated as though his life
doesn't matter
How much love can one have to give to a murderer of the
undeserving
Cold-blooded DNA
The hate didn't come from nowhere
No, it's been there
For almost as long
As love.

ABOUT THE AUTHOR

John is the author of the first two volumes of an ongoing book series entitled *Motivation for the Masses: A Poetic Autobiography, A Collection of Collections*, and on many occasions has served as a Keynote or Motivational Speaker and Poet. John was born in East Point, Georgia and grew up there, College Park, and Clayton County as well as Memphis, Tennessee. After attending Clayton State  University, he took an opportunity to work for the Department of Defense as a civilian and live in Iraq and Qatar supporting our troops during Operation Iraqi Freedom. As a result, John developed a passion for world travel to accompany his longtime passion for writing and reciting poetry. During that time, he also started a career in Information Technology and has since served as an Engineer and Subject Matter Expert in the discipline of Microsoft Infrastructure Systems for many organizations ranging from small to enterprise. In 2013, he formed The Dilworth Group and began providing IT training and consulting services, first to high school and college students in Clayton County, GA and then on to a wide variety of

B2B customers. He currently resides in Atlanta, Georgia as he continues his endeavors as an entrepreneur, investor, and motivator of people. John believes his God-given purpose in life is to motivate people to Learn from their mistakes, Appreciate their blessings, Think optimistically, and Use what they've been blessed with to be a blessing to others; his primary method for carrying out that purpose is through living as an example. John enjoys his newfound love of golf, his appreciation for cigars, an insatiable diet of reading, and genuine love with his friends, family, and fellow citizens of the world.

@JOHNFDILWORTH

JOHNFDILWORTH.COM

A free ebook edition is available with the purchase of this book.

To claim your free ebook edition:
1. Visit MorganJamesBOGO.com
2. Sign your name CLEARLY in the space
3. Complete the form and submit a photo of the entire copyright page
4. You or your friend can download the ebook to your preferred device

A **FREE** ebook edition is available for you or a friend with the purchase of this print book.

CLEARLY SIGN YOUR NAME ABOVE

Instructions to claim your free ebook edition:
1. Visit MorganJamesBOGO.com
2. Sign your name CLEARLY in the space above
3. Complete the form and submit a photo of this entire page
4. You or your friend can download the ebook to your preferred device

Print & Digital Together Forever.

Snap a photo

Free ebook

Read anywhere